Praise for Imagination First: unlocking the power of possibility

"*Imagination First* offers a blueprint for tapping into the power of imagination, which is the core of innovation. To maintain our competitive edge, we need to balance instruction, encouraging our children to be creative and to develop their imaginations Every student should be in a classroom where investigating, questioning, and discovering are inherently part of the curriculum. In today's economy, these skills are essential for success and continued world leadership in the 21st century."

—John I. Wilson, executive director, National Education Association

"*Imagination First* is a wonderfully written book that makes a powerful case for how much we owe to imagination. And it is full of detailed, useful suggestions for how to release that powerful force in each of us. It couldn't be more timely!"

—Mihaly Csikszentmihalyi, director, The Quality of Life Research Center

"Drawing from literature, the latest science, and a wide array of real-world examples, *Imagination First* shines a much-needed lantern into the blackbox of the creative process. For anyone interested in succeeding in today's imagination economy, this timely book offers an expansive and accessible toolbox."

—Daniel H. Pink, author of *A Whole New Mind* and *The Adventures of Johnny Bunko*

"*Imagination First* is an excellent primer for everyone: business leaders, scientists, inventors, you name it. The "real-world" practices I found here are invaluable, supported by case studies in education, the arts, business, and sports. The authors demonstrate that there is a reservoir of imagination in each and every one of us waiting to be tapped in order to succeed—and excel—in this competitive world. An incredible book."

—Ben Silverman, co-chairman of NBC Entertainment and Universal Media Studios

"Imagination—we all want more of it. The question is, can we teach it, and if so, how? Eric Liu and Scott Noppe Brandon answer yes, and they chart the way in this engaging and delightful book. Our kids will be the better for it!"

—Joel I. Klein, chancellor, New York City Department of Education

"This is a wonderful book about opening our minds, by two writers who understand well what is likely to close them. Each chapter demonstrates how to break the bonds of unseen assumptions, by 'rinsing out expectations,' redesigning spaces to support generative conversations, creating new narratives, and much more. Each chapter is just long enough to deliver a mind-popping idea and just short enough to keep us from getting lost in our usual thoughts."

—Rosamund Zander, author of *Art of Possibility*, family therapist, executive coach

"*Imagination First* unlocks the secrets of the most important aspect of human consciousness and will be a valuable aid to anyone wishing to unfold their potential for creativity."

—Deepak Chopra, author of *Reinventing the Body, Resurrecting the Soul*

imagination
first

imagination
first

unlocking the power of *possibility*

Eric Liu and
Scott Noppe-Brandon

JOSSEY-BASS
A Wiley Imprint
www.josseybass.com

Published by Jossey-Bass
A Wiley Imprint
989 Market Street, San Francisco, CA 94103-1741—www.josseybass.com

Jossey-Bass books and products are available through most bookstores. To contact Jossey-Bass directly call our Customer Care Department within the U.S. at 800-956-7739, outside the U.S. at 317-572-3986, or fax 317-572-4002.

Jossey-Bass also publishes its books in a variety of electronic formats. Some content that appears in print may not be available in electronic books.

Library of Congress Cataloging-in-Publication Data
Liu, Eric.
   Imagination first : unlocking the power of possibility / Eric Liu and Scott
Noppe-Brandon.
      p. cm.
   Includes bibliographical references and index.
   ISBN 978-0-470-38248-6 (cloth)
1.   Imagination. 2.   Creative thinking. 3.   Originality. I.   Noppe-Brandon, Scott. II.
Title.
   BF408.L74 2009
   153.3--dc22
                         2009023241
Printed in the United States of America

First Edition
HB Printing   10 9 8 7 6 5 4 3 2 1

Contents

Contents (continued)

Contents (continued)

Contents (continued)

Acknowledgments

Imagination First emerged from many overlapping
collaborations. We'd like to thank some of the people
we've worked with while creating this book.

First, we want to thank all the remarkable people we
interviewed and visited in the course of our research.
Spending time with them made this a transformative
process for us. Similarly, we'd like to thank the equally
remarkable participants of the many Imagination
Conversations sponsored by Lincoln Center Institute and
by the Guiding Lights Network. The ideas and insights
they shared in these nationwide public events shaped our
approach in important ways.

Lesley Iura, our wonderful editor at Wiley/Jossey-Bass,
has been an imaginative and open-minded guide and
partner. She has great instincts and a discerning eye, and
we're so fortunate that she *gets* it. The design, production,
and marketing teams at Wiley/Jossey-Bass are dedicated
professionals, and we thank them as well for all their
efforts.

In the Lincoln Center orbit, we'd first like to thank Reynold Levy, the president of Lincoln Center for the Performing Arts. He has been a great champion of LCI—and of the larger endeavor to bring the potential of imagination to the forefront of public understanding. Deep thanks also are due to Ann Unterberg, chair of Lincoln Center Institute, and to Bonnie B. Himmelman and Susan Rudin, its vice chairs. We'd like to honor Loet Velmans, who underwrote the creation of the LCI Imagination Award, for his support and vision.

Maxine Greene, LCI's philosopher-in-residence, has been a source of inspiration for many years. Her legacy as thinker, teacher, and role model is deep and we're grateful to her. Thanks to Madeleine Holzer, Cathryn Williams, and Alison Lehner-Quam for their inspired leadership at LCI; specifically, Madeleine for her work in naming the Capacities for Imaginative Learning, Cathryn for expanding LCI's reach across the nation and abroad, and Alison for her vital collaboration in this book and indispensable management of the process.

We salute LCI's staff, teaching artists, and partnering educators, all of whom shape LCI's practice and worldview. Among the great LCI staff who've helped make this book possible are Ashleigh Blomfield, Julia

Clark-Spohn, Linda Miles, Sasha Papernk, Jennifer Poggiali, and Christopher St. Clair.

From the Guiding Lights Network, we want to call out and thank all the luminaries and partner organizations who've been part of the Guiding Lights Weekend every year and part of our other activities such as the Creativity Matters summit and the School of Life. The Network folds in many wonderful people blessed with many forms of imagination, and that is especially true of the core team who make the Weekend possible: Claudette Evans, Jená Cane, and Alex Martin.

Scott wishes to thank his wonderful children, Jesse and Geordy Noppe-Brandon and Zach Brandon, for teaching him that being playful and serious are not antithetical; and his beloved wife, Gail, for her unmatched ability to make words dance and ideas flow. Eric would like to thank his mother, Julia Liu, and his daughter, Olivia Liu, for showing him so many ways to keep his mind and heart open; and Jená Cane, for being, in every sense, his partner in possibility.

Last but not least, because this has been (and continues to be!) a truly rewarding collaboration, we'd like to thank each other. Having the right cocreator on a project like this spells the difference between work and play. Creating *Imagination First* has definitely felt like play. Onward!

Lincoln Center Institute

Learning to Ask: What if . . . ?

Lincoln Center Institute for the Arts in Education
(LCI), established in 1975 and located in New York City,
is the educational cornerstone of Lincoln Center for the
Performing Arts, Inc. Over its thirty-five years of existence,
the Institute has grown as a provider of arts in education,
and has long been a leading organization in developing
skills of imagination through guided encounters
with the visual and performing arts. LCI is driven by its
conviction that the imagination is an essential cognitive
skill that can and should be taught, but also—and
crucially—that imaginative thinking and learning are
vital in today's global society, not only in the classrooms,
but in the workforce as well. More than ever, in a world
that struggles to adapt to its vastly different points of
view while facing a difficult economic time, the Institute

feels that it is its responsibility to propagate the idea of imagination, creativity, and innovation as indispensable tools of survival for all: artists, scientists, entrepreneurs, mathematicians, politicians, or business leaders.

From Ideology to Action

In the course of its practice, LCI's educational approach has been shared with more than twenty million students, teachers, college professors, and arts administrators representing public schools, arts organizations, and professional teaching colleges in New York City, across the nation, and around the world. To bring the attention of the larger community to the new perception of the imagination, LCI has taken many important steps. These are some of its creations and initiatives:

- Whole-school efforts range from the founding of new public schools and traditional and charter schools to the restructuring of schools from large to small, from theme-less to theme-based. By "whole-school," it is meant that the Institute's methodology of imaginative teaching and learning, anchored by the Capacities for Imaginative Learning, is applied throughout the curriculum, to every subject, in every class.

- The Imagination Award is given annually to a New York City public school that epitomizes the best practices of integrating the arts throughout the curriculum and an imaginative approach to teaching and learning. This initiative has been adopted by the State of Washington.

- Imagination Conversation events are organized across the nation. These conversations bring together professionals from diverse disciplines, technology industries to journalism, who look at the impact of imagination in their work and their lives and share insights on how best to apply practices in the classrooms that support an education for imagination.

- The Capacities for Imaginative Learning are a medium that acts as a series of guideposts for teaching and learning. The Capacities, detailed in this book, are now one of the most important elements in the teaching practices of schools involved in what is known as aesthetic education.

- In 2008, the Institute launched a series of online courses in professional development that center around the digital work of art designed by artists of the OpenEnded Group using the body and movements of choreographer and dancer Bill T. Jones.

- An annual performing arts repertory of dance, music, and theater works is renewed each year by LCI and presented in hundreds of performances at Lincoln Center and on tour to local schools. Visual arts are explored through exclusive photographic portfolios, works in the local museums and galleries, and selected architectural sites.

- Lincoln Center Institute National and International Educator Workshop, Online Courses, Summer Session, and Teacher Education are among LCI's year-round professional development opportunities.

- Lincoln Center Institute Consultancies are custom-designed professional development workshops for schools and districts, arts organizations, and universities.

Economic competitiveness, quality of life, educational advancement, and civic education—more and more, these are associated with capacities of the imagination. Leading those who call for a change in our educational strategies is Lincoln Center Institute. Its work is in the process of shifting the educational paradigm, and therefore, we hope, influencing the mindset of the nation seeking to prosper in this century.

See www.lcinstitute.org for more information.

The Authors

Eric Liu is an author, educator, and civic entrepreneur.
He is the founder of the Guiding Lights Network,
dedicated to the practice of mindful and imaginative
mentorship. His previous books include *Guiding Lights:
How to Mentor and Find Life's Purpose,* the official book
of National Mentoring Month; and *The Accidental Asian:
Notes of a Native Speaker,* a *New York Times* Notable
Book. He is also coauthor, with Nick Hanauer, of *The
True Patriot.* Eric served as a White House speechwriter
for President Bill Clinton and later as the President's
deputy domestic policy adviser. He speaks regularly at
conferences, campuses, and corporations. Eric now lives
in Seattle, where he teaches at the University of
Washington and serves on the Washington State Board of
Education.

Scott Noppe-Brandon, executive director of Lincoln
Center Institute, has spent the past fourteen years proudly
leading the arts and education branch of the world's
foremost performing arts center, Lincoln Center for the
Performing Arts. A practicing educator and performer

prior to taking the helm of the Institute, Scott is known internationally as a speaker, writer, and advocate for education in and through the arts. Over the course of his career he has helped start and revitalize numerous public schools, contributed a column to *Education Update,* and authored or edited numerous books and articles on the arts and education. Currently, he is leading a campaign to conduct Imagination Conversations—summits of leaders from all walks of life who care about fostering a culture of imagination—across the United States.

Learn more about Eric and Scott at www.imaginationfirst. com.

imagination
first

The Premise

Scenes of the Crime

et's imagine three scenes.

Imagine an eight-year-old girl growing up on a ranch in eastern Washington state. Imagine her as she steps into the yard under the clear night sky, after all the chores are done and the dishes washed, and begins constructing a vision of herself aloft, amidst that starry train. She searches for plumes of fire. She picks out the luminous object that moves. She tracks its arc across the dome. She swells with purpose and resolve, and walks across the moonlit grass back into the house to tell her father that when she grows up she is going to be an astronaut. He snorts, and says with a killing chuckle, "That's no life for a lady."

She never leaves the atmosphere.

Imagine a biologist working at one of the country's great cancer research centers, doing what he calls "high-end bricklaying" in a large scientific project funded by a large government grant. One day his infant daughter dies. The death is sudden, unexpected. He is distraught. He goes into a dark, deep hole, and finds that the only way out of the hole is to think about mortality. Or rather, immortality. He reads science, fiction, science fiction. He reads myth, religion, poetry. He comes out of the hole with a clear vision. He can no longer just do his bit part in a large endeavor of someone else's making. That's normal science. He needs his own project. On how to stave off death, to borrow enough time so that someone who suffers sudden trauma, who slides quickly toward death, can be treated, healed, saved. He goes to his division director and says *I have to be able to do my own thing here at the lab or I have to leave.* The director ponders this and says, "I'm sorry you feel that way but if I let you do this, I have to let everyone, and I can't do that." The biologist blinks.

He goes back to bricklaying.

Imagine a young but not-so-young-anymore man who's been working at the same family services nonprofit in Harlem for ten years, running it for the last five. There's a lot he can be proud of: lots of individual kids he's helped, lots of thankful notes from parents who needed that helping hand. But something is gnawing at him, and it's a sense that there is a bigger invisible web, an inactive latticework around him, and his efforts are not connected to it. He can build his little tiny bulwark and protect his tiny cohort from the tide, but all that means is the tide swells more heavily to his left and to his right. He reflects, he asks, he listens, and then an idea comes: he will make that web visible, that latticework active. He'll tie together all manner of social service agencies, and leverage public dollars, and he'll save not just a few kids here and there—he will save a whole generation in Harlem. He will break a cycle. He goes to his board and says he wants to create a cradle-to-college ecosystem of community initiatives that will educate parents to be parents and let Harlem's children be children. The board puts him off, asks him to focus on the job at hand.

He stays in his corner of the web.

In each scene, a kind of murder was committed. Each story was marked by the calculated or offhand killing of a person's sense of possibility.

Now, imagine if in each instance something had gone differently.

What if that eight-year-old's father had nodded with encouragement? What if he'd given even silent assent to her ambition? What might've happened? Well, she might've turned out like Bonnie Dunbar, a pioneering NASA astronaut and space shuttle crew member who would inspire countless young people and would later become director of the National Museum of Flight.

What if that cancer researcher's boss had said, "Yes, I think you can do this and I think you should"? What might've happened then? He might've turned out like Mark Roth, who won a MacArthur fellowship in 2007 for his discovery of a method that uses tiny doses of toxic gases to literally suspend animation in mice and small mammals, and allows them to be reanimated without ill effect. His company, Ikaria, is developing the method for human application.

What if that nonprofit entrepreneur had had the courage of his convictions? He might've turned out like Geoffrey Canada, the creator of the Harlem Children's Zone, one of the nation's most ambitious and original efforts to change the lives of poor, forgotten black children, and an initiative that President Obama aims to replicate across the country.

In her essay "A Room of One's Own," Virginia Woolf asked us to imagine that William Shakespeare had had a sister, every bit as talented a poet as her brother, every bit as attuned to the nuances of human interaction, every bit as inclined to step onstage and express those nuances— but barred: barred from exercising or cultivating her imagination by the sheer accident of her gender; mocked when she dared express a desire to write plays; turned away at the theater. The tale of this hypothetical sister is not only the tragedy of womanhood; it is the universal tragedy of untapped talent, of imagination fully seeded but never sprung.

Think about your own life. Find a moment, from five minutes ago or five decades ago, when someone or something killed your imagination. Chances are, you can't stop with one. Chances are, you can create a roll call of such internal deaths. Our unsung, unread autobiographies are littered with them: an unkind word from a boss, a sneer of mockery from friends, a painful penalty for coloring outside the lines, a threatened and threatening look from a spouse.

Or think of broader patterns in our society. Everywhere we turn, the scene is littered with evidence of the killing of imagination.

Fifty million Americans without health insurance. The Lower Ninth Ward still in tatters. Public schools that every day leave millions of poor children behind. Fragmented families and communities. Unchecked man-made climate change. A sharp decline in American patents, scientific research, and economic competitiveness. A total debt that outstrips our nation's productive capacity.

Each one of these persistent problems sits like an open sore on the body politic, visible to all and never healing. Our habit, as citizen-spectators, is to behold these failures and to speak of them as failures of *will*: to assert or assume that Americans no longer have the national life force, the willpower that we had last century, to face these problems head-on and to solve them.

But in fact, these are not primarily failures of will. They are failures of imagination. We had stopped imagining, as a people, what it would look like if every American had the health care needed to live as a full human being. We generally do not imagine a Lower Ninth Ward where the nation applies sustained attention and resources and where stability and opportunity emerge. We struggle still to imagine public schools that truly keep the promise of a fair shake for all who start life with the least.

The general assumption is that a will to act must precede imagination—that you decide to do something before you imagine what it is. The reality is that imagination comes first. It must. Until and unless we have the emotional and intellectual capacity to conceive of *what does not yet exist*, there is nothing toward which we are to direct our will and our resources.

Nelson Mandela first *imagined* a multiracial democracy when all around him on Robben Island was only the stony monolith of apartheid. *Then* he summoned the will to outlast the monolith. J. K. Rowling first *imagined* a world of wizards and limit-bending acts of magic when all around her was only the harsh scarcity of welfare and single motherhood. *Then* she put her vision to the page, fully realizing that world and conjuring from mere wisps of inspiration a very real juggernaut of a media franchise.

A New Path

Every one of us lives in a world shaped by what social scientists call "path dependence," which is what happens when an institutional arrangement gets locked in and becomes self-reinforcing. The classic example of this is the QWERTY layout of the keyboard. The first typewriters were clunky and prone to jam, and so the awkward QWERTY layout was invented to keep certain common letter pairs from clashing. Why do we have it still? Because it became an industry standard early on and it got entrenched. An economist might note that the "switching costs" of changing to a more intuitive keyboard today are too great. But the truth is, almost nobody even *contemplates* the possibility of a friendlier format. We do things the way we do them because that's the way we do them. The lock-in effect is a great enemy of imagination—and this is true everywhere, not just in keyboard design. Life is filled with QWERTYs.

And it's becoming more difficult than ever to tolerate them. We live in a time of tremendous and accelerating change, at every fractal scale of society. Everything, in ways both empowering and disorienting, is now fluid: Our ability to define our personal identities in an authentic way. Our ability to make and remake our families. Our ability to find neighborhoods that give us a sense of place rather than isolation. Our ability to make our work meaningful and our enterprises purposeful. Our ability to sustain a sense of common cause as the nation separates centrifugally into ever-finer social slivers. Our ability to master, rather than be mastered by, globalization and its consequences. Our ability to expand the meaning of *our* and *us*.

At each scale, the challenge is the same: How do we unlearn a habit of helplessness and acceptance? How do we see each moment as a potentially critical juncture for new possibilities, rather than part of a foreordained flow? How do we see ourselves as agents rather than victims of change, or even its passive beneficiaries? How do we learn to see with new eyes what is, what could be, and what must be? The gating factor here is not willpower; it is nonblindness. The obstacle is not just path-dependence but also path-*acceptance*.

When the 9/11 Commission wrote its final report and recommendations, it described a litany of failures: of planning, implementation, follow-through, communication, coordination. But the most damning failure it enumerated was a failure of imagination. The government had failed to imagine that terrorists might strike at America in such a stunningly symbolic, asymmetrically powerful way. Perhaps an analyst here or a case officer there had conceived of the possibility that this could happen. But the government—the collective of analysts and officers and policymakers and citizens—had not conceived of it and consequently did not prepare for it. "Imagination," the Commission observed drily, "is not usually a gift associated with bureaucracies." And so its telling recommendation was that going forward, our intelligence agencies had to learn to "routinize imagination."

Routinizing imagination is not the work only of heroes— the geniuses, the luminaries, the elect. The work belongs to every one of us. Nor can this work come merely in response to crisis. It must come every day. What's most revelatory about the study of imagination is, indeed, the everydayness of it. Imagination can be embodied in its most developed forms by a great figure or in great history-bending acts. But we believe that enduring, systemic change comes when every one of us develops, in an abundant bloom of acts and choices, at work and home and play, our own mindfulness about being imaginative. We can all use imagination across every part of our lives—and we can all learn to do it better.

Albert Einstein conducted thought experiments that enabled him to make leaps that other scientists of his time—even great ones—could not. It wasn't that Einstein had lots more determination or computational brainpower than his near-contemporary Henri Poincaré, who came tantalizingly close to many of Einstein's most famous insights. The difference, according to biographer Walter Isaacson, was imagination: from the time Einstein was young, he practiced visualizing things in novel ways. What would it be like, he asked himself, if you could run alongside a wave of light? What if you were in an enclosed elevator accelerating up through space? By starting with such questions and playing with them, instead of accepting the "givens" of normal science, Einstein was able to take his already prodigious mind and open it even more. And thus was birthed his theory of relativity.

Any conceptual breakthrough requires imagination first. We don't have to be Einstein to see this—or to conduct thought experiments of our own, about whatever matters most to *us*.

We start by deciding to take note of our blindness. We proceed by inquiring about its origins. We grow by developing new ways to see and reroute our perceptual apparatus. Imagination can unfold in the conscious and deliberate and in the unconscious and intuitive. It unfolds in flights of fancy and in hands-on play. It can emerge from crisis or from calm. *Routinize* imagination?

We don't know whether it's possible to do that, at the
CIA or anywhere. But the charge is inspiring. And it'd be
a crime not to try.

What We Aim
to Do Here

This short book has a simple purpose: to show you that
it's possible to develop and cultivate imagination—at
every concentric circle of human endeavor, from the
personal to the global—and to show that we have no
choice but to do so.

This is not a frivolous book. Some books on the topic of
imagination or creativity try a little too hard to be
creative. They sprinkle the text with loopy doodles, funny
fonts, and random asides to show just how wacky this
topic can be. In our view, such an approach can
sometimes reinforce in the reader the misplaced belief
that *I'm not one of those creative types*. It can marginalize
imagination even as it tries to make it accessible.

At the same time, this is not a "heavy" book. Some books
on the topic of imagination or creativity try a little too
hard to be serious. They litter the text with scientific
argot, data-filled graphs, and double-blind studies to
show just how substantive and nonflimsy this topic can
be. In our view, such an approach can reinforce in the

reader the reaction that *all this academic jargon dresses up the truth—either you got imagination or you don't (and I don't).*

We've read shelves of both types of books. What we're trying to do in these pages is offer another choice, an approach that neither places imagination on a pedestal nor trivializes it.

We believe that a developed imagination matters profoundly to the health and promise of our society. We've got an argument to make about that and some myths to bust. We also believe that imagination can be cultivated, and that everyone—*everyone*—can raise their level of imagination and readiness to apply it. Put those two beliefs together and you get a third: that it's time for our society to get going on an intentional, dedicated, and systematic effort to up our imagination quotient—the *real* IQ—at work, at home, in school, at play, and in our community life.

We come to our beliefs through experience and collaboration. Scott has for fourteen years led Lincoln Center Institute, the educational arm of the world's leading performing arts center. LCI has been unlocking the imagination of children and teachers for decades and, through its Imagination Awards for courageous public schools and through nationwide Imagination Conversations, it is, popularizing and democratizing the idea. Eric, after serving as a speechwriter and then a senior policy adviser to President Clinton, has helped spark a national movement around mindful mentorship through his book *Guiding Lights.* The Guiding Lights Network convenes experiential conferences on the art of imaginative mentoring, bringing together leaders from business, education, politics, and other walks of life. We've cross-fertilized efforts for years. We believe in a pedagogy of possibility.

There are three parts to this book: the *premise,* the *practices,* and the *purposes.* This first part lays out our overarching argument and vision: what we mean by imagination and "imagination first"; the myths that we need to clear out of the way; why imagination matters so much; why we nevertheless resist it.

The second part is focused on what can be done in the face of that resistance. It lays out a set of twenty-eight-and-a-half practices, much like a field manual or a handbook. We culled this list from our two years of research on this project—countless sessions of watching, talking to, and playing with practitioners from all over the country and from all walks of life. And the third part distills themes from all these practices and then asks what we aim to *do* with all this imagination.

We like our list of twenty-eight-and-a-half practices. And maybe you'll like it so much that you'll conclude they capture all there is to say about how leaders, parents, teachers, and managers can spark and stimulate the imaginative capacities of the other human beings in their lives.

Rather more likely, though, you'll find that our list is just grist—that it inspires you to append, amend, revise, and create. You'll have four or forty more ideas to add, and some to delete. That's why we've created a Web site—imaginationfirst.com—where you can describe your *own* practices and where you can add or revise ideas in an open-source spirit.

So consider this small volume the start of a conversation. And consider yourself now one of many coauthors of a never-ending book.

What, Why, and How

What Imagination Is

t might be helpful at this point to define some terms.

We define *imagination* simply as the capacity to conceive of *what is not* — something that, as far as we know, does not exist; or something that may exist but we simply cannot perceive. It is the ability to conjure new realities and possibilities: in John Dewey's words, "to look at things as if they could be otherwise."

Often, the words *imagination* and *creativity* and *innovation* are used interchangeably. We see things quite differently. We see these three concepts as related but very distinct phases of a continuum.

If imagination is the capacity to conceive of what is not, then creativity, in turn, is imagination *applied*: doing something, or making something, with that initial conception. But not all acts of creativity are inherently innovative. In our view, innovation comes when an act of creativity has somehow advanced the form.

For example, if a child thinks of a ten-foot flower, she is exercising her imagination. If she sits down and actually draws that flower, she's exercising creativity. But only if that drawing is an advancement of the form of drawings of flowers can she be said to have innovated. In our sequence of *imagination, creativity,* and *innovation*—we call it the ICI Continuum—imagination comes first.

Imagination → Creativity (imagination *applied*) → Innovation (*novel* creativity)

That's not just in the temporal sense. We believe that of the three elements, imagination is foundational and the most important, and demands proportionate attention. Imagination is the sine qua non. Without a healthy and well-fed imagination, there is no creativity or innovation.

Although imagination matters most, it gets the least ink. Libraries have shelves of volumes about creativity, orders of magnitude more than can be found on imagination. And whenever there are public conversations about these topics in business, politics, education, and the arts, most people focus on the final phase of the ICI Continuum.

Every day, a hundred corporate retreats and school board meetings and civic forums are all focused on the holy grail of innovation. We want innovation! Now! We want the magical ten-foot flower! Never mind the seed or the water or the sunlight. Or the vision, in the first place, to turn a parking lot into a garden.

This book has a point of view, and it's that there is no such thing as instant innovation. Imagination comes first, and it demands of us patience and intentional, mindful cultivation. In a sense, this is a gardening book—both a paean to the garden and a guide to tending your own.

We have a corollary point of view, which is that imagination matters even if you don't care a whit about innovation. That is to say, the true utility of imagination is measured not by some ratio of innovations-per-ideation. It is best measured by whether the ecosystem as a whole is richer in possibility, and whether the society we feed with our imagination enables all participants in the market or the community to participate to their fullest potential.

It is not just a semantic distinction that we are making with our ICI Continuum. The distinction underscores, rather, why it's vital to examine imagination per se: the quality and durability of any creative act depend in great measure on the fertility and force of the imagination that feeds the act. This is where it all begins. We reap what we sow.

What Imagination Isn't

But first, some weeding.

There are three common—indeed, paralyzingly prevalent—myths about imagination, repeated so often that they have long acquired the ring of truth: first, that you either have it or you don't; second, that how imagination works is a mystery; and third, that it therefore can't be taught, instilled, developed, or cultivated. Before we go on, we must debunk them.

You Either Have It or You Don't

This is the most persistent and damaging myth. Implied by this canard are the notions that some of us simply don't have imagination, and that whatever amount of imagination we may have is a fixed quantity that never changes. Both notions are demonstrably false. Imagination is the raw ability to conjure up a different reality. If a person can dream, then he or she can imagine. If people can ask "what if" or move in the world "as if," then they have imagination. Period. If an institution's culture and leaders encourage the pursuit of new possibilities, then that institution has imagination. The challenge is how to increase the potency and reach of that imagination. And so it is necessary next to debunk the idea that imagination is a fixed and static entity. One of the exciting things about recent advances in cognitive science is that they confirm what any parent knows intuitively: that if you inculcate certain habits. form a certain kind of environment, provide certain kinds of models and stimulants, then you can palpably increase the size and elasticity of a toddler's imaginative muscles. So it is for learners of any age, individually and collectively. Imagination is completely malleable: we all have it—*and* we can all develop it.

Imagination Is a Mystery

There is a certain poetic truth to this statement, but when you get down to it, it is a cop-out. Although it's impossible to reduce the creative process to an algorithm, it doesn't follow that we should throw up our hands and treat it as a black box, or that we should reduce ourselves to mere spectators while the few "geniuses" among us practice their inexplicable forms of imagination. Alex Osborn's 1953 book *Applied Imagination,* which pioneered the very idea of "brainstorming," reminds us that we all can demystify both the process of imagination and the application of imagination. And yet people from all walks of life are habituated to saying that imagination is like intuition: a gut thing, beyond words and rational understanding. Of course, as Malcolm Gladwell has shown in *Blink,* intuition itself is becoming less of a mystery each day. But the deeper problem is the romanticizing instinct. What if we took such a romantic and incurious approach to, say, researching and combating cancer? Imagine if we said that *because* past a certain point we don't understand why certain cells metastasize, we should *therefore* not explore what we can and develop all the tools we can to fight cancer. It's a lot easier to bury our heads in the sand than it is to create a fine-grained image of what really goes on inside our heads.

Imagination Can't Be Taught

But of course, the resistance to the idea that imagination is teachable does not come only, or even primarily, from our heads. It derives, uncontrollably, from the heart. We often fear imagination. The fear has many facets, and it can take the form of personal paralysis or institutional inertia. Some of us fear that we have too barren a store of dreams, images, ideas, and examples to add up to anything. Some of us fear what will happen to us when people around us dream more interesting and expansive dreams. To be truly imaginative is to run to the right when everyone else is running to the left to defy convention and reject the comfort of conformity. Some of us fear such isolation. Others of us may grant that imagination can be cultivated, but fear that we do not have the cultivating touch. And then, perhaps most of all, some of us fear the necessary consequence of admitting that imagination can be taught, which is admitting that most of us *choose* not to become more imaginative. Facing that fact—that we are the authors of our own stuckness—can be terrifying. But it is a fact that litters business school case studies and postmortems of all kinds of failed organizations. Fortunately, there are countless examples of people who have devised simple, smart, and repeatable ways of unlocking other people's imagination, and of weathering the maelstrom of fears that follows. And they have figured out how to take these insights from a personal scale to the organizational. Every day these people practice imagination—and pass it on.

The inverse of these myths—that everyone does have imagination and can increase it; that imagination can be understood and therefore improved; and that it can be taught and cultivated—provides a good summation of our worldview.

Why It Matters

Having grasped more firmly what we mean by imagination, you might now ask: How does this abstract topic play out in real life? Why, really, should we care? In this section, we want to conjure up a few scenarios that make plain the role of imagination in our everyday lives.

Why imagination? Because the vitality of our economy depends on it.

The New Commission on the Skills of the American Workforce paints an ominous picture of the surge in skilled labor in China, India, and other emerging economies—juxtaposed against an aging American workforce that needs serious retooling. In every sector, our competitors' investments in education and technology are eroding the edge that has traditionally justified the pay of American workers. As China and India climb the skills ladder, there is, in the view of the Commission, only one potential competitive advantage left for Americans: our imagination.

A capacity for imagination cannot be outsourced. It is our greatest domestic renewable resource. But by the same token, a nation that allows its stock of imaginational capital to erode is in trouble. It is announcing, in bold type and at volume ten, that it wishes to be dependent rather than independent, a bystander to great forces rather than the creator or master of those forces. If there is greatness to America—and we insist there is—it has always derived from the unseen seed of imagination, not from the conspicuous fruits of that seed (wealth, power, beauty, bling). We are transfixed with the fruit. We need more seed.

There's a story that a computing pioneer said in 1943 that there would be a worldwide market for about five computers a year, given how expensive and massive the machines were. As we play with our smartphones today, we can chuckle knowingly at the myopia of such a statement. But then—*smack!*—we will walk forehead-first into the next wall: the wall of our own assumptions and illusions, a wall that reminds us how much we are inhabitants—dare we say prisoners?—of what we imagine currently to be reality.

Is the next economy going to be driven by green tech, nanotech, biotech, space tech? Maybe. Or maybe it will be driven by something else right in front of us and yet in effect invisible, obscured by the veil of our own expectations and by conventional definitions of opportunity. No one can dictate what the next innovations will be. But unless we feed our collective capacity for imagination, we can be sure that those innovations will be fewer and farther between.

Why imagination? Because our ability to engage a world in flux depends on it.

Back in 1994, the author, historian, and consultant Daniel Yergin wrote a book called *Russia 2010* Yergin and his coauthor Thane Gustafson have a firm called Cambridge Energy Research Associates and they are in the business of scenario generation. Their clients ask them to come up with possible geopolitical futures, and to play out the business and social risks and opportunities in each. Writing at a moment when a new post-Soviet Russia was in its awkward uncertain infancy, Yergin and Gustafson posited three possible Russias fifteen years on: a destitute failed state; a neo-Communist regime; and a Western-facing phoenix with benevolent economic might. As it turns out, none of their three scenarios played out. What has played out, here on the eve of 2010, is a hybrid of all three with healthy dollops of stuff they never contemplated.

The point is not that *Russia 2010* is therefore worthless. To the contrary, it is priceless—because it is an example of trying to conjure up what does not exist (when most of us don't even bother to attend to what exists now), and because it reveals that often the best way to suggest an infinitude of possibilities is to suggest a finite number of them. How does Iraq turn out in fifteen years? How does the tribal region at the Pakistan-Afghanistan border turn out? How do China's growing wealth and inequality change its approach to democratic governance? How will Russia's oil wealth and nuclear weapons play out in great power politics?

No one can say with certainty, but that does not absolve us of the responsibility to say with uncertainty. We have to be willing to start somewhere.

Why imagination? Because it opens up the way we try to forecast the future.

Because it's not enough to extrapolate forward from what we know today. On ESPN's Sportscenter, the exuberant Chris Berman makes weekly NFL score predictions in a segment called "Swami Sez." Each week the Swami tells you that the Seahawks will beat the Giants 24–13 or the

Chargers will wallop the Broncos 33–21. He also tells you how accurate his predictions have been so far in the season. Give him credit for that. But like most forecasters, Berman doesn't ever review why his wrong predictions turned out wrong, and like most forecasters, he makes each round of new predictions by doing what mutual-fund fine print warns us against: betting that past performance predicts future results.

And so what goes into his predictions is how the Giants looked on offense last Sunday, or what emerged in practice this week about who's banged up or not. Never does the Swami say, "The Giants will win this week because their Pro Bowl linebacker will blow out his ACL in the first quarter and the backup will rack up record sack totals." Never sez Swami, "The Hawks will eke out a victory tomorrow because in the waning seconds, a referee will be standing in the wrong place and what would have been the opponents' game-tying touchdown pass will glance off his shoulder and out of bounds."

You can't blame him for not saying this. How could he? But how much fun would it be if he did. And how enlightening! Not as prediction but as preparation. For these are precisely the kinds of events that so often determine the outcome of a game. And this is true no matter what the game is. What the onetime derivatives trader Nassim Nicholas Taleb calls "black swans"—the rare random events that we never plan for or build projections around—turn out often to be epochal market-defining, game-changing events.

Wouldn't it help us, then, in every arena, to look at causation with more open eyes? It would help us break the chain of denial and mutual delusion that led to the housing bubble and its swift and catastrophic collapse. It would help us see how all the stakeholders in any project have their own swirling orbits of cause and effect that distort how they move in the world. It would make us more aware of what the true matrix of relationships is that envelops us. It would enable us to anticipate more, or perhaps to replace the stress of trying to anticipate with the realization that what makes any sport joyful is randomness. But there is one thing absolutely necessary for such clear-eyed exploration of causation. And that is a capacity in the first place to imagine the black swan.

Why imagination? Because without it, education is utterly empty.

Today's culture of testing and data collection in education was born of a good intention: to close the persistent achievement gaps of race and poverty. But over time, ends and means have sometimes gotten muddled. Too many public schools focus on the measurable to the exclusion of the possible. As a result, too many students end up better prepared for taking tests than for being skillful learners in the world beyond school.

All is not bleak, of course. We've witnessed firsthand a rising number of inspired schools in New York City, Washington state, and across the country where a "Dragnet-style education"—*just the facts*—has been replaced by a passionate commitment to critical thinking and imaginative learning. The challenge now is to replicate such success stories so that they become the new norm.

We can start by dispensing with the notion that there is a zero-sum conflict between imagination and accountability. Sometimes this notion is posed as a fight for finite resources: *There's barely enough time for basic content and you want us to do imagination too?* Other times it's posed as a fight between ideologies: *While you prattle on about imagination and nurturing the student's creativity, the kids are failing to learn the basics.* But this is an utterly false choice. The more our schools focus on imagination—in curriculum, in teaching practice, in school design—the more they will achieve the results for which they're being held accountable.

Why? Because imagination isn't a nice-to-have luxury in education. It is, rather, what makes education relevant—to *everyone*. Giving teachers and students and principals a chance to apply their imaginative capacities makes all of them much more motivated to be in school. Back to basics? In our view, there is nothing more basic and fundamental in good education than developing the innate ability to imagine. Start with that base, *and then* add in the math facts, the history facts, and the essay-writing formulas. When all we do is focus on the content and not the skills to manipulate content, we are not producing scientists or artists or investigators for the twenty-first century. If we merely cram kids full of a lot of *what,* we leave them utterly unready for *What If.*

This is an ironic moment: American classrooms are becoming more like those in East Asia—test-minded and drill-dependent—while educators from Shanghai and Singapore and Seoul are coming here to figure out what makes American students more flexible than theirs, more capable of improvising and transitioning from one situation to another and remixing old bits of knowledge into new ideas. They think we foster imagination and creativity in America. We do. That is our culture. And that is what we need to remember when we try to envision great schools. We don't need to become more like Asia. We need, as James Fallows wrote during the height of the 1980s fear-and-emulation reaction to Japan's rise, to become *more like us.* Committed to imagination.

Why We Fear It

What if. Are there two more powerful words?

They are children's words, to be sure. We both, Scott and Eric, have children. And we both remember being children. We love it when our children play games of *What if*. And in the pages that follow, you'll hear plenty about how we can develop the imagination of all children.

But these two words—*What if*—are also seriously adult words.

Sometimes that means they are treated like curse words: inappropriate, impolite interruptions of a tacitly agreed-on pact of satisfaction with the way things are. Sometimes the words are treated like indulgences, wasteful distractions, or vulgarities deserving swift rebuke: people recognize the power of *What if* but so deeply fear its unseen might that they dare not release it.

Any of this sounding like your office? Your school? Your organization? Your family? Your circle? Your *people*?

What makes *What if* seriously adult is that these two words turn out to be the key to successfully performing the experiment called being human. For what separates us from the beasts—and from the best artificial intelligence programs—is that we humans have a capacity to bootstrap from *What is* to *What if*. In fact, it is this capacity, and our ability to express it in word and image, that makes human consciousness the miracle it is.

And yet, most of the time most of us squander this absolutely miraculous pile of genetic lottery winnings. We are born with imaginations that, if developed, could run like Porsches, but we move through the world like Model Ts. In spite of our wondrous capacity to take our perceptions of the world and convert them through analogy, induction, and recombination into something imagined, not yet extant, counterfactual—in spite of our capacity to see a pile of horse manure and to imagine a pony in there somewhere—it turns out that most people prefer a known situation that is bad (standing beside that stinky pile) to an unknown situation that could be dramatically worse (diving deep into it) even if the situation could also be dramatically better (finding a pony!).

This illuminates the problem. *What if* is scary. *What if* encompasses not only the possibility that the world is round and circumnavigable but also the possibility that it is flat and drops off abruptly to Hell. As children we will tolerate the latter possibility. Indeed, as children we revel in it. And then, as we become adults and as we become socialized to certain norms of mutual justification (I won't challenge the flimsy façade that is your social identity if you won't challenge mine), too much threat gets bound up in any consideration of the scary possibility. As adults, we accumulate reputation and status and power more quickly than knowledge or awareness. As adults, we have too much to defend.

And so we live with what we have.

How to Push Through

We believe the best way to push through this resistance to change is to offer a useful set of practices Our approach is influenced by people like Donald Schön, author of the seminal work *The Reflective Practitioner*. Schön, who was a great student of learning, articulated the notion that to be a professional was not merely to master a set of technical skills but also to *practice* like an artist. He meant this both in the sense of dedicated rehearsal and in the sense of calling. Practice matters. To see oneself as pursing a purpose and following a call, rather than merely going through the motions, is itself an act of imagination. And critically, it is an act of reflection. Schön calls it *reflection-in-action*. What are we doing? Why do we do what we do? Why do we repeat what we have done? Facing ourselves honestly, and in fellowship with others, is the first way to combat the resistance and fear that grip us when a better way beckons.

But we believe that a companion approach to combating such resistance is in fact *combat*. Fighting the fear of *What if* is an endeavor with certain martial aspects. And so, perhaps not surprisingly, we were also influenced by a trio of works that employ metaphors and methods of warfare. Sun Tzu's *The Art of War*, in the Oxford edition translated by Samuel B. Griffith, is one: it equips us not only with axioms of strategy but with an actionable mindset, to fight always the battle beneath the battle. Then there is Steven Pressfield's *The War of Art*, a potent collection of maxims reminding readers that to be an artist of any kind—be it in the arts or sciences or politics—is to gird oneself for a ruthless, disciplined dismantling of second guesses, deep-seated fears, and big blocks.

Perhaps most surprising was the way we were informed by a more recent book, the latest edition of the *U.S. Army/Marine Corps Counterinsurgency Field Manual*. This is the book created by General David Petraeus, whom it made famous and who later commanded all American and allied forces in Iraq. What was inspiring to us was not the substance of the book—though in its pages Petraeus did bring a more jujitsu-savvy and history-minded approach to counterinsurgency—but rather the format. The manual, in crisp bites, sums up generations of lessons learned. Here is a set of concise practices for field commanders, prefaced by a theory of action for policymakers.

We looked at that and said, "That's what we want." It struck us that it is precisely for a topic like imagination, seen by so many as airy and ephemeral and *soft*, that a forceful, evocative handbook for practitioners is what's needed.

Informing our approach throughout is a set of meta-skills that Lincoln Center Institute has over the years developed and refined for the Institute's work in the schools. These "Capacities for Imaginative Learning" derive from the work of LCI's renowned philosopher-in-residence, Maxine Greene, and from the practice of countless artists and educators in the Lincoln Center orbit. The theory of action behind these Capacities is that close engagement with a work of art (or any object of study)—whether a poem by Coleridge or a postulate by Copernicus— unleashes a student's ability to think of and express new possibilities.

It's instructive to list the Capacities here (in slightly revised wording to apply beyond the classroom). Particularly in this form, they underscore how universal and accessible every aspect of imaginative learning is:

- **Noticing deeply**—identifying and articulating layers of detail through continuous interaction with an object of study

- **Embodying**—experiencing a work through your senses and emotions, and physically representing that experience

- **Questioning**—asking "Why" and "What if?" throughout your explorations

- **Identifying patterns**—finding relationships among the details you notice, and grouping them into patterns

- **Making connections**—linking the patterns you notice to prior knowledge and experience (both your own and others')

- **Exhibiting empathy**—understanding and respecting the experiences of others

- **Creating meaning**—creating interpretations of what you encounter, and synthesizing them with the perspectives of others

- **Taking action**—acting on the synthesis through a project or an action that expresses your learning

- **Reflecting and assessing**—looking back on your learning to identify what challenges remain and to begin learning anew

These habits of mind and heart were designed originally for arts and education, but it is our firm belief that they are guides for life. They are the DNA of this book, threaded through its practices and stories. Look for the Capacities as you read; we won't always call them out. Then look for them as you live; they won't be called out there either. Can you attend to the complexity of things beneath the surface? Do you know how to listen with your full body? How to notice recurring patterns? How to interpret them and act on them? Do you know how to reflect back on what you experienced?

As you move into the second part of this book, you will meet many people from many places who will be your companions, guides, and exemplars. You'll go to the pods at the MIT Media Lab where the future is invented, to the labs near Disneyland where Imagineers work, to the Fred Hutchinson Cancer Research Center, to *The Lion King* on Broadway, to Whole Foods, and to Marine Corps Officer Candidates School. You'll learn about cognitive science and gestalt psychology, theater direction and star-mapping, video game design and negotiation strategy. In these imaginary travels, and in all the practices we present to you, everything will connect to everything.

The twenty-eight-and-a-half practices that follow are a beginning, not a be-all and end-all. Some overlap, some echo others. Themes arise, some even intentionally. There is a loose arc to the list but nothing sacred about the sequence. The descriptions combine anecdotes and more general principles, but the anecdotes are meant to serve as fodder for your own analogy making: take them where you want to. Or let them take you where you don't want to. Apply the general rules to your particular terrain. This is a field manual, a toolkit. We've done our best preparing it. Now we invite you to make something of it.

part Two

The Practices

Make Mist

Ready, get still, go

W e like to think that life is action—that living is moving, that animation is what generates *anima*. But in fact stillness is a most fertile breeding ground for ideas. The problem is, modern life is almost completely free of stillness. Our hyperkinetic culture tries to colonize it, treating stillness as just one more flavor of stimulation to choose from or one more task to accomplish. But making it a "to do" doesn't do it; that only tightens the grip of our control-freak multitasking minds.

Whole Foods founder and CEO John Mackey, who conceived of the idea of an organic grocery chain, says, "Scheduling is the enemy of imagination." As often as possible, in good quarters or bad, he will clear his calendar for days at a time. During those blank hours, he reads. He thinks. He gets lost in science fiction, economic theory, comic books. He notices where resistance arises, where inspiration flares. He's not *trying*, Mackey insists, to cultivate imagination. There's no plan. He merely trusts that letting things unfold nonlinearly is the best approach to growth that is enduring and, well, organic.

Laurie Coltrin, one of the Imagineers who create the attractions at Disney theme parks, places similar faith in stillness. A freak snowstorm in Florida as the premise for a ski ride at Disney World? Sure! Her job is to bring that crazy idea to life, and to translate it into a masterwork of space and place. And how she starts is by going to what she calls "the misty place." She sets her alarm early and stays in bed half awake, letting strange and loosely formed ways of seeing things float past. As the mist of these dawndreams moves in, she notices what it curls around and rises above. The mist tells its own tale.

David Gonzalez, master storyteller, knows this well. Gonzalez creates wildly inventive multimedia monologues for the stage. His acclaimed productions can have multiple moving parts: big bands, irresistible dance sequences, primordial myths brought to life with gesture and elliptical suggestion. It takes a great deal of energy for Gonzalez to make the parts fit and flow onstage. But before he does any of this—the harvesting, the mixing, the matching, the orchestrating, the revising, the improvising—he first makes a conscious effort to meditate in solitude. He shuts up, and allows what comes to come. He forgives what won't come if it won't. He knows he's a story whisperer before he's a story teller.

What these three share is trust: in silence, in themselves, and in the logic of magical thinking. Sometimes, to be sure, imagination is sparked by frenzy. But frenzy is generally not a sustainable life strategy. Far more fruitful is the practice of simple stillness. Quiet the mind. Unplug. (A BlackBerry has no icon for imagination.) Do one thing at a time. Then do no thing at a time.

Leave the Campfire

Know your enemy: it is you, scared

Fear kills imagination. And fear is always with us. Pretending it doesn't exist might work in a pinch, but eventually it returns. Learning to name, face, grapple with our fears: this is the start of the art of everything.

Because imagination is related to images, and images are related to the brain, it is logical to think of imagination as a purely cognitive capacity. But imagination is equally about emotion. It is about the animal instincts of fight or flight. It originates in the gut, in the chemical explosions that precede conscious thought. When you can overcome fear, you earn a chance to exercise your imagination. When you can't, you don't.

Can you imagine being in charge or being your own boss? Can you imagine writing that novel you've dreamed of? Can you imagine striking out on your own? Can you imagine not being *stuck*? If you can, you are mastering one set or another of fears: of failure, exclusion, isolation, mockery, loss of face or status or power. Of punishment for not following the rules.

Most people prefer the certainty of the mean to the risk of the extremes. Most people have no idea where their power actually originates. One of the hallmarks of the entrepreneur is a willingness to go one way when 99 percent of people go the other. As the technology investor and serial entrepreneur Nick Hanauer puts it, "If everyone thinks something is a good idea, it's either not a good idea or it *used* to be one." But it's harder than it looks to be that solitary contrary person. Mere independence of mind is not enough. Fundamentally, it demands a habit of knowing what you are scared of. Taking stock of those fears. And then, being purpose driven enough to push through.

Think of any creative act—Steve Jobs deciding to create the first computer with a graphical user interface, Nixon making a secret overture to communist China—and reverse-engineer it. Before there is the daring product or performance, there is an imaginative vision. What bridges the two is a persistence in the face of naysaying, a willingness to say at critical points, "I may be scared but I can see a new way and I choose to proceed."

When Mark Roth, the researcher we met earlier who suspends animation, decided he was no longer going to do traditional scientific research and was instead going to embark on an uncharted course of inquiry about immortality, he knew well that he was "about to leave the campfire," as he puts it. The campfire represents the safety of community: in a dark and uncertain realm, this is where you can huddle for warmth. But it also represents the oppression of the crowd: walking away from the campfire sets in motion a reaction of defensive self-justification from those still there. *You're not leaving us; we're ostracizing you!*

When Roth sensed that reaction from the huddle, he realized he had to get very clear about how he defined success and failure. His fear of drifting off the grid of respectable science was great. But he took measure of his fear. In so doing, he saw that his desire to search out the boundaries of immortality—a desire born of tragedy, and thus infused with meaning and motivation—was greater than his fear of going down an intellectual blind alley. And he began to explore. All along the way, and even now that his wanderings have led to great discoveries and a MacArthur genius grant, he still likes—needs, it seems—to retrace the arc of his journey.

The telling matters. The choreographer Twyla Tharp has a ritual to banish the paralyzing fears that can prevent her from imagining, let along creating. She calls it "a staring-down ritual, like a boxer looking his opponent right in the eye before a bout." Once she decides to leave the comfort of what she already knows, once she determines it is time to venture out alone, she reckons that demons await. And she makes a disciplined habit of confronting them. She writes down what scares her about the next endeavor. *People won't like it. I won't know how to do it. I won't be able to live up to my reputation.* One by one, she knocks those demons down to size.

For Roth as well, there was no trick for overcoming fear except confronting it, naming it, and then telling people why he did what he did. It was in that telling and retelling that Roth sharpened not only his story but also his sense of what mattered most. Ultimately, he did not obliterate the fear that was stifling his imagination. He simply trumped it with something stronger: a sense of purpose. And so can we all.

Flip What's Foolish

Make it wise to be foolish, and every fool will generate wisdom

t's remarkable how much and how early we are socialized not to be fools.

One thing that reflective practitioners of imagination know how to do is to perform mass jujitsu. If the prevailing attitude is that standing on your head is foolish, they set a tone that says *not* standing on your head is foolish. What was out of bounds yesterday, weird, wrong, or inappropriate, is what's expected today. More to the point, what was safe, normal, and appropriate yesterday is now deemed foolish. These practitioners unleash imagination by inverting inhibition and creating permission.

Perhaps one of the most exuberant of such figures is the Boston Philharmonic conductor and leadership guru Ben

Zander, whom Eric wrote about in *Guiding Lights*. One of Ben's favorite methods of countering the fear of appearing foolish is to get his perfectionist students, whenever they make an error, to stand up with a broad smile and arms outstretched and proclaim with gusto, "How fascinating!" Sometimes those perfectionists are musicians at the New England Conservatory in the middle of rehearsal, sometimes they're CEOs and world leaders preening at Davos, sometimes they're kindergarteners already learning not to color outside the lines. Ben doesn't care.

And such cultivated carelessness is the point. *How FAS-cinating!!* Try it. It takes a few times to get past the giggles of inhibition and then it is incredibly liberating. Because it's true: the things we do wrong are usually, like it or not, pretty fascinating. Our work doesn't always have to be so perfect.

Timothy Gallwey, the tennis coach and author of the classic *The Inner Game of Tennis,* coined a famous distinction between Self 1 (our natural, freely moving embodied self) and Self 2 (our chattering, relentlessly self-judging critic-over-the-shoulder self) and he designed tennis exercises to get Self 2 to shut up. In one such exercise the tennis student has been hitting balls in-bounds for a long time and then is abruptly invited to hit the ball on the other side of the white line—that is, on the side formerly known as "out-of-bounds." Now, by encouraging the student to hit it there, by removing the white line of the stigma of judgment, Gallwey frees the student to remember what it's like to *play*.

We cultivate imagination and make its exercise possible when we create permission to nudge what had once been foolish into the realm of the OK.

Of course, context matters. Gordon MacKenzie, in his charming book *Orbiting the Giant Hairball*, tells of his years at Hallmark, where he was, in effect, the designated fool. His job title was "Creative Paradox" and oddly, that describes the company itself: Hallmark generated its revenue from the creativity of its cards, but as an organization it could be stolid and inhibited. From time to time, one Hallmark division or another would invite MacKenzie to lead a workshop on how to be more imaginative and creative. He had great ideas and he tells some hilarious stories about his ingenious methods.

But intentionally or not, MacKenzie reveals how ultimately enervating it is when organizations decide they need to "assign" someone—whether in-house or external—the role of the fool. The foolishness consultant. When permission is granted this way—like a pill prescribed, a fluid to be injected—it has few lasting effects. In the end, it only reinforces the preexisting frame of what's allowed.

Foolishness is not an object to be acquired. It is an ongoing negotiation over an ever-shifting boundary. We, collectively, get to decide what is permissible. That is imagination. So the trick is this: to give people permission to give *themselves* permission. This approach, rather than command-and-control permission, is scalable. And it turns out—as Zander knows and bosses like MacKenzie's forget—that the best way to do it is to model it yourself.

Make Way for Awe

Nurture humility and the wonder that comes with it

There is nothing like knowing it all to kill the imagination. When we become expert, or think we have, we get the benefits of intellectual shortcuts and far greater processing efficiency—but we suffer the cost of closed-mindedness. Having seen it all, we stop looking. Having been there, we stop going. Having done that, we stop doing. To rekindle the imagination we would do well to rediscover the sense of awe—of wonder—that every child comes equipped with and that seems to seep out along the trip to adulthood.

For instance, take a trip to a small inflatable dome in Asheville, North Carolina.

There you'll find David McConville, a young devotee of Buckminster Fuller, the polymath inventor of the geodesic dome. Like his role model, McConville is part artist, part scientist, part dreamer, and part tinkerer. McConville and his team, fed by eclectic apprenticeships in astrophysics, event production, and multimedia engineering, invented something called the GeoDome. Maybe fifteen feet across, eight feet high at the peak. As portable as a tent, as immersive as a womb. Step into the darkness, feel your way to a little canvas camping chair, be seated and gaze upward.

Here begins an experience of pure wonder. Using Google Earth, real-time NASA data, state-of-the-art animation designed by a Pixar veteran, a single laptop, a projector, and an Xbox joystick, McConville takes the guests on a journey to . . . anywhere they want in the known universe.

Start here on Earth, outside of New York, say, and zoom out to the moon, to the edge of the solar system, past the Milky Way's far tendrils, headlong into a snowstorm of other galaxies, a storm that goes on and on. Oh, back to Andromeda? No problem. Next, flip a switch and visualize the magnetosphere and the assault of energy unleashed by the sun on the Earth. Another button illuminates the surprising swarm of satellites and space junk orbiting our planet. Fly toward the constellations, see the stars of Orion's Belt as we learned them in school, as dots to connect, painted on the ceiling. But then turn the perspective 90 degrees and now see the belt sideways, in 3-D: it thrills and embarrasses to realize that the three stars of the belt are not remotely on the same plane. Now, at full dizzying speed, back to the polar icecaps of our planet, where visualizations à la *An Inconvenient Truth* show various scenarios of glacial melt.

This is not your father's planetarium. This is a fountain of youth.

The GeoDome inspires childlike awe not only because of its stunning visual effects but because, as an experience, it collapses all possible scales of worldview and time frame. When you're zigzagging up and down the *z*-axis, from earth-scale to galaxy-scale to ecosystem-scale to universe-scale, you get a self-directed, nonlinear version of the famous Eames documentary *Powers of Ten*. The effect of this metaphysical migration is to impress upon the traveler the ultimate inseparability—indeed, interchangeability—of every scaled slice of space and time.

McConville's firm, Elumenati, made the GeoDome a dome on purpose. "We want you to feel like the universe is being re-enchanted," he says. "With a screen, there's you, and then there's the world inside that rectangle. A spherical view is truer to what we actually perceive. It acts more like an inner subjective. The dome, being a dome, is in essence a representation of our imagination."

Awe matters. McConville uses the GeoDome to stir policymakers into action about climate change, to light up schoolchildren about space and the stars, to educate laypeople about the interdependence of everything. As he narrates his tour of the cosmos, statements like "We are made of stardust" become deeply moving, nearly spiritual insights. He's not dazzling us with rocket science (though there's plenty of that); he's simply unleashing our capacity for awe. Our gratitude for that makes us ready and willing to learn.

John Seely Brown, former head of Xerox PARC lab and now an avid chronicler of advances in digital learning, describes a "golden triangle" of inspiration, imagination, and innovation. At the heart of the triangle is awe. "Awe drives imagination," he says. "A great teacher can take a plum and see magnificence in it." Imagine, then, a GeoDome for a plum. Imagine a GeoDome for the world as an ant sees it, or as a photon of light sees it. "What does it mean to be able to hold the world in awe?" asks Seely Brown.

That's for you to know . . . and for you to find out.

Reinvent the Wheel

Be willing to give back the givens

S ome things we take to be laws of nature, or works of mankind long ago perfected. Take the wheel. If ever there was a cliché about creative work, it is that we should at all costs avoid "reinventing the wheel."

But at MIT's Media Lab, a team of researchers is doing just that. Literally. As part of their Cars in the 21st Century project, these scientists have designed automobile prototypes in which all wheels operate independently. Instead of being connected to a common transmission and drive train, each electrically powered wheel, like a little robot, contains its own motor, suspension, brakes, and steering mechanisms. This will allow next-generation cars to maneuver more nimbly and, by eliminating the traditional linkages to the engine and passenger compartment, it creates the possibility of radically different shapes of cars—configurations that save energy and conform more naturally to the body.

Will it work? Will we see these cars anytime soon? Who knows. But the audacity of the endeavor is thrilling—both for the *what* of it and for the *how*.

In a delightful series of experiments on how ideas get generated, psychologist Thomas Ward asked subjects to imagine and draw animals from other planets. Initially, people batched aspects of "animalness" the way they are batched on Earth: the imaginary creatures were bilaterally symmetric and had two eyes and two ears and two or four legs. This was true even when they were told the alien planet was very different from our own. Ward calls this a "structuring effect": what we know constrains our ability to imagine what we don't know.

But when Ward told the subjects to consider what the alien planet's environment looked like and what features the creatures would need to survive there, the results were much more imaginative and novel and they deviated much more widely from Earth exemplars. By taking the discussion up one level of abstraction, thus widening the scope of context, Ward was able to help his subjects widen their range of possibility.

Whenever we find ourselves, then, bumping up against the "structuring effects" of our own past experience, two moves should come to mind: consider the wider environment and, once there, treat nothing as sacred.

This is just what the MIT team did. After all, they didn't set out consciously to prove they could make a better wheel. They had, rather, a greater goal in mind: reconceiving the car for an era of overpopulation and energy scarcity. In the course of pursuing that goal, they simply were able and willing to question and reinvent everything. Including the wheel.

Our instinct is not to solve problems by expanding them. It is to confine and contain them. But there are times when expanding the frame enables you to be less attached to what had seemed preordained or perfected—the *givens*—in the smaller frame. With detachment, a simple insight emerges. Most givens can be given back. And perhaps even more exciting, you get to decide which ones to keep.

Think Inside
the Box

Make greedy, grateful use of limits

In our culture today, everyone is told to think outside the box. Put aside the question of how much original thinking can be going on if everyone is rushing outside the box. Even in Lake Wobegon, we can't all be nonconformists. The real question that arises when we hear this advice is, *What's wrong with the box?*

It turns out that boxes—that is, limitations—can be incredible prompts to imagination. In the Seattle fringe theater scene, there is a biannual pressure cooker of creativity called "14/48, The World's Quickest Theatre Festival." Every winter and summer, over the course of forty-eight hours, fourteen ten-minute plays are conceived, written, scored, rehearsed, and performed. On Thursday night, seven playwrights are given a theme—mistaken identity, say—and the next morning they come back with a play that the actors, tech crew, director, and musicians scramble to bring to life. Repeat, with seven new playwrights, Saturday. These command performances are remarkable for how much beauty and hilarity they randomly generate.

At Marine Corps Officer Candidate School, they do something similar. One of the most grueling and revealing tests that the young candidates go through is called the Reaction Course. You are assigned to lead a team of four. You are brought to what looks like a small makeshift playground, with, say, a barrel, some rope, a high wall, what looks like a gymnast's uneven bars, and two wooden poles. The instructor paints a scenario: one of your team has been severely wounded and you must devise a way to transport him across a gully, represented by the uneven bars. You have fifteen minutes. Go.

The instructors are watching, clipboard and timer in hand, to see how the team leader leads under pressure. The Reaction Course might well be called the Revelation Course, for it quickly reveals whether you're a delegator, a controller, a listener. Do you suffer from paralysis by analysis? Do you rush into an attempt without thinking it through? Do you let someone else take charge? Do you defend your authority at the expense of good ideas?

There is no right answer to the challenge; in most cases, there may be no solution possible in the time allotted. Maybe the two poles can be turned into a stretcher. Maybe the ropes and the barrel can be used to make a pulley. Maybe the wall can be used like a fulcrum. Maybe one of the poles can be—*time's up!*

The genius of the Reaction Course is that it uses severe limits, of time and material, not only to test the temperament of the team leader but, more fundamentally, to awaken the leader's openness to new ideas. Limits beget inventiveness. Limits force open the imagination. As in 14/48, the intensity and accelerated incubation of ideas can yield inspired works and performances.

Pick up a little pamphlet published by the toy and game company MindWare, called "101.3 Ways to Create Imaginative Solutions." It's the Reaction Course for kids, using household items. Open up to any page and it will say something like, "For the five challenges listed here, you may use any of the five following items: Macaroni, Shoe Box, Rubber Bands, String, Cardboard." Then scenarios follow, such as, "You have recently become aware of a major burglary in your local museum. Formulate and demonstrate a superior alarm for a museum." Or "Devise a method to automatically count the number of coins in a pile."

When the celebrated architect David Rockwell was a child, with his widowed mother working in vaudeville and a parade of performers streaming through his life, he became fascinated with communal play. He looked at the world around him and saw on the beaches and in the attics and by the roadsides the stuff of carnivals and black box theaters and haunted houses.

Years later, he noticed that his own children enjoyed playing more with the cardboard box that a new art table came in than with the table itself. The stunted, risk-averse plastic playgrounds of our era no longer capture the imagination of children. They'd rather just have a box. Rockwell began to conceive of a new kind of playground: unstructured, free, child-centered, and consisting almost entirely of raw ingredients. Loose parts made of wood and metal, sand, some water, multiple levels of platform and ground. "Playing with sticks," Rockwell observes, "reminds us that in the best play there are no permanent artifacts." There's just some stuff, and imagination.

The adventure playground movement that Rockwell has helped pioneer places no time limits on the play. But by stripping down the materials to their basic essence, this new breed of playground reminds us that limits can be our friend. (Rockwell now has designed "Imagination in a Box" kits for adults, based on the same principle.) The critical factor is *intention*. Our lives are boxed in by limitations, material and attitudinal, that we inherit or create. It takes intentional practice to see those limitations not merely as something to tolerate but as the source of new invention. When we can convert scarcity into an asset, we are not just playing well. We are living well.

Hoard Bits

Collect obsessively; sift; trust that the right bits will emerge

"I was not naturally talented—I didn't sing, dance, or act—though working around that minor detail made me inventive."

So writes Steve Martin in *Born Standing Up,* his illuminating chronicle of how he became a stand-up comedian (and why he stopped). Martin describes a course that was, as he puts it, "more plodding than heroic." In his ritual of post-show self-evaluation, he meticulously charted what worked each night, what didn't, how he made use of deficiencies like lights that didn't work or unplanned boons like an arrow-through-the-head prop that happened to be in the box. Being a great and inventive comic, in this instance and likely many more, has a lot to do with having a Benjamin Franklin–like obsession with methodical self-improvement and a mania for collecting, classifying, assessing, and reapplying bits.

Bits are everywhere. The director Julie Taymor, creator of the stage version of *The Lion King* and numerous films ranging from the Frida Kahlo biopic to a Beatles-inspired romance, always wanted to be a cultural anthropologist. At Oberlin College she acted and directed in student productions, but her academic life was devoted to folklore and ancient cultures, and traveling to places where she would always be the watchful outsider, filling her mental and artistic storehouse without order or taxonomy. Here were masks from Bali, stage arrangements from medieval Christian passion plays, billowing fabric from the Beijing Opera, visual frames from Fellini. She didn't think of it in terms of filling a storehouse. There was no conscious method to it. But in fact, the more she collected, the deeper the pool of techniques, motifs, and conventions that she was able to draw from, and the richer the amalgams she was able to invent on stage and screen.

There is method to the madness of the pack rat. One of the Disney Imagineers' mantras is *Gather, store, recombine.* When Imagineer Owen Yoshino had to come up with concepts for an adaptation of Space Mountain in Tokyo Disneyland, he thought, wouldn't it be great if a ship could levitate? That led him to remember a robot cartoon from his childhood, in which the robots used magnets to hover off the ground. That led him and his team to experiment with magnets to allow the space vehicle to levitate. "I'm a huge pack rat," Yoshino admits. He'll take anything—old cartoons, propaganda posters, erector sets—and stash them for use some other time. His office is crowded with the artifacts of research field trips.

But Yoshino's point is that you don't need official field trips to see anew. You just need to open your eyes. The cognitive scientist Ronald Finke has conducted fascinating experiments in which people are provided images of elemental shapes—cones, pyramids, bowls, blocks, tubes—and asked to come up with as many combinations of shapes as they can and then to invent as many useful objects as possible. The interesting finding is not that people are capable of great inventiveness; they are. The interesting finding is that their imaginative capacity is most powerfully activated only when they've been exposed to these "preinventive forms," as Finke calls them. Collecting the forms and bits and then messing with them in combinatorial play—without a specific goal in mind—leads to inventions and insights "that seem so elegant and resourceful in retrospect." But mainly in retrospect. At the front end, it's about being a pack rat and trusting your pile.

When singer-songwriter Paula Boggs composes, she is drawing half-consciously from a vast trove of riffs and passages, compiled over a lifetime of voracious, multigenre music listening. "It's only later," she reflects, "when someone else hears it and tells me they heard a Motown or a rhumba moment, that I realize where it came from." Boggs' instinct to collect and combine—and to allow new insights to emerge from a diverse pool of elements—turns out to serve her well in her day job, as general counsel and executive vice president at Starbucks. There, as onstage, she sees connections—between people, ideas, products, deals—that aren't obvious. She can imagine more combinations than many others can.

Our brains are naturally associative. So our job is to feed them material to associate and synthesize. And then to give ourselves tasks where association is called for and even rewarded. Lego works this way: you hoard as many kinds of pieces as you can, so you can be prepared to make whatever you need or want. Now imagine a Lego set containing not Lego pieces but rather everything in the world: a vast library of all possible modes of thought and action. Now imagine not playing with those Legos in solitude but in collaboration with others.

Whether it is a physical cabinet of wonders or a treasure trove in the mind, the place where the bits are hoarded is never inert. It beckons. It inserts itself into your life. It suggests combinations. All you have to do is keep filling it with more, and more diverse, stuff than you think it could ever hold. Take inventory of it from time to time. And then let it take inventory of you.

Mix Your Metaphors

Change the metaphors that frame your reality

oes man make the metapho–s or do metaphors make the man?

When a school is designed like a facto–y, people behave accordingly. But how would they behave if we thought of the school as a well-tended garden?

When the economy is conceptualized as a closed, self-correcting equilibrium system, people behave accordingly. But how would they behave if the market were seen as a garden?

When a family is understood in terms of cycles that can't be broken, people behave accordingly. But how would they behave if the family were a garden?

"[T]he way we have been brought up to perceive our world is not the only way and it is possible to see beyond the 'truths' of our culture," assert George Lakoff and Mark Johnson in *Metaphors We Live By*. This cult classic is a compendium of the ever-ramifying concepts, small and large, that are the proteins of our cultural DNA . . . or the currency of our interpersonal exchanges . . . or the glue that holds a society together. You get the point. By highlighting such basic and prevalent metaphors as ARGUMENT IS WAR or TIME IS MONEY or LOVE IS A JOURNEY, they aim to make visible the countless ways we construct our reality with metaphor. All seeing, in a sense, is *seeing-as.*

We need metaphors because the world is complicated. Metaphors package and chunk up the chaos of everyday experience into clusters we can use to understand, to communicate. But after a while, we stop seeing the distinction between the metaphors and the reality they signify. "The blind acceptance of the metaphor can hide degrading realities," write Lakoff and Johnson.

So what should we do? Not just reexamine our metaphors but mix them. Deliberately. Listen closely when someone mangles a metaphor: why did they do that? Learn how other cultures using other languages express human experience in their own distinct metaphors. Consider alternatives to your everyday metaphors. Imagine alternative genealogies for your everyday metaphors.

Replace your most commonly used metaphors with a new all-purpose one like ___ IS A GARDEN. Gardens grow. They require weeding and feeding. They yield hybrids. They grow organically, but left to themselves they go to seed. Or consider ___ is a GIFT. Now fill the blank with ARGUMENT, TIME, or MONEY. Could you imagine an argument being a gift?

To make it fit, you have to ask: What does it mean to give a gift? What does it mean to have a gift? What are the *properties* of gifts? And this, ultimately, is the heart of the exercise: when we make a metaphor we are transferring the core properties of one thing (the source concept) to another thing (the target concept). To enrich our imagination, Lakoff and Johnson teach us, we have to go back to the source. We have to ask what properties we would like to see more of in our lives (generosity, community). We have to consider what things contain those properties (gifts). And then we have to make those things the lenses through which we take in the world. We have to retrain how we see. Because it turns out that LEARNING IS SIGHT.

Renew Your Narrative

Ask whether your story still serves you

What is identity but a nested set of narratives? There is the narrative of who you are as an individual, the narrative of who you are in family, of your tribe or group, of what you are capable of doing—or not.

We are predisposed—hardwired, according to neuroscientists—to make sense by making narratives. We wish to conceive of ourselves, as Joseph Campbell has written, not as a spectator in the game of life or even a protagonist but as a kind of hero. Narrative is the frame upon which we hang selected swaths of experience in order to construct a shelter of meaning. With story, we have a sense of place. Without story, life feels like chaos.

The narratives that frame our lives can be creation myths, or explanations of how things work, or justifications of why things are. A life-forming narrative can lurk in the undeveloped images and deleted scenes of our dreams. It can announce itself quite self-consciously in our codes of everyday interaction. It can be a nursed grievance or a rendezvous with destiny, an etching of the past or a vision of the future. It can be all these things. Whether based on reality or not, our narratives *make* our reality.

Sometimes our inextinguishable human need to fit facts into an overarching story can serve us well, infusing our lives with purpose and a sense of call. *I am meant to help people during challenging times.* By placing us in a context larger than ourselves, narrative can embolden us to be our fullest selves. *Music is my gift and I will pursue it even if it's impractical.* It can reinforce our better angels. *My people have suffered greatly, so we are doubly compassionate toward others.*

But sometimes—indeed, sometimes simultaneously— our need for narrative can imprison us. When the narrative we have made is along the lines of *I am a self-made man (and you should be one too)* or *Our team always chokes at the critical moment* or *I'm worthy because I can endure punishment,* then it can become dangerously confining. Sometimes, out of duty or peer pressure, we adopt a myth at odds with our nature or aptitudes. *I'm a brawler like my father before me.* And when it curdles into something like *I have been screwed over and I will make others pay,* it can become pathogenic.

Few things impede the flow of imagination like dead narratives—narratives that block our ability to grow, that have outlived their usefulness but accrete and calcify. When that happens, as the dream expert Robert Moss says, "We bind ourselves to the wheel of repetition, because we refuse to reimagine our situation."

The first thing to do, then, is to halt the whir of the wheel and to become aware of our narratives, collective and individual. If we become attentive to the stories we tell about ourselves, the symbols and memories and defining moments that we unconsciously align into an all-encompassing story, then the matrix suddenly becomes visible. We step to the threshold of self-awareness.

Once at that threshold, though, we have to be willing to act. Ask yourself: Is this story I tell confining me? Is it allowing me or my circle to live at our fullest potential? If it is not, then a new mindset is in order. A remodel of your narrative, a reconstruction of that house of mind.

We are so often raised to believe something profoundly limiting: that traits such as imagination or courage or intelligence are, to use Carol Dweck's words, fixed entities. We come to believe that either you have it or you don't, and the amount you have is the amount you have. Dweck, a Columbia University psychologist, points out in her pioneering research that a mindset of fixity is cruelly self-fulfilling. When you tell yourself a story that you just aren't good with numbers or strangers or machines or conflict, you pretty much make it so. That is, imagining yourself to be limited makes you limited—because you give up trying or practicing when you hit the first obstacle or get your first negative outcome.

But Dweck's research offers an alternative narrative: no matter what your starting abilities in any realm, with applied effort you can elevate your game. And it turns out that believing *this* is also self-fulfilling. That is, imagining intelligence or courage or imagination to be something you can shape and increase helps make you—with practice—more intelligent, courageous, and imaginative.

It all depends on the story you start with.

Untie Your Tongue

Talk about your work with someone who doesn't understand it

The astrophysicist Luke Keller often spends his days staring at sheets of colored vertical lines—spectrum graphs that mark the presence and the age of light reflected or emitted by celestial bodies. His work is to imagine the story that those lines tell about the origin of the universe. Sometimes it's hard to extrapolate backward that way. More often, it's easy—in the way that reading an EKG becomes easy and automatic for an experienced physician. But just as a doctor can sometimes miss the critical story lurking in the jagged lines of the quickly scanned EKG, so can an astrophysicist miss the point of those spectra.

So Keller has a regular practice whenever he feels the need to shake up his thinking. He speaks in tongues.

Not literally, mind you. But what he does is talk about his field with people who don't have the language for it. To these audiences, his scientific language is incomprehensible. He may as well be speaking in tongues. And this forces him to unwind his jargon and, in the process, to unpack his assumptions and retrain. So, for instance, he from time to time visits his daughter's preschool class. He brings a basketball to class and drops it and then asks the kids what happened. They don't talk about gravity and mass and acceleration. But they do ask why a ball can't fall up. And that opens Luke's mind.

When Luke teaches his introductory course at Ithaca College, he keeps open ears for the naive questions his students pose. "Where does dust come from?" they will ask. "What came before a star, and how do you know?" And as he works hard to answer such a question in language that can bridge to the students' understanding, he realizes he needs to ask the very same question of his expert colleagues. So later on he will call up another high-powered astrophysicist and ask in all earnest, "Tell me again how a star forms?" Not because Luke forgot or doesn't know, but because he knows too well. He needs to notice anew all his jargon and shorthand.

His knowledge, once expressed in new ideas and clear words, is now more tacit and intuitive. And it's only in the course of refreshing that most basic vocabulary— rearticulating from the bottom up—that he finds himself able to approach his own cutting-edge research with true imagination. As he reminds himself how to tell this story so that a child could understand it, he reminds himself that there are many more ways to interpret data than he has let himself see. By loosening the tongue, he opens the mind.

Then it's back to the spectrum graphs.

Swap Bodies

Lose yourself in a role

Z ack Brock is one of the most buzz-generating young musicians on the jazz scene. He plays the Blue Note, the New Orleans Jazz Fest, pizza joints in Brooklyn, art galleries in Austin, you name it. He plays violin. Trained classically and raised by a pianist mom and a dad with a weekend garage band, Brock has had many musical influences. He had a great Montessori teacher who told stories in an enveloping, enrapturing way. He had a mentor, Daniel Bloom, who made Brock obsessive about interpreting music through the prism of architecture, and practicing for mastery of the weight, density, and span of sound. He reads voraciously. He is a movie buff. He is an omnivore of improvisation: baroque ornamentation, bebop, stand-up comedy. In short, his bits runneth over. But the best way Brock opens up his channels for improvising and inventing—indeed, the way he first leapt into the world of jazz—is to go deep into role play.

"At a gig," he says, "I'll set a goal: 'Tonight I'm an alto sax player.' And I will truly believe with all my mustered energy that I'm not playing the violin." What results is as transporting for his audience as it is for Brock. The power of such role playing is not just that it generally limbers up creative muscles. The true power lies in the fact that by surrendering to such a role—and on another night's gig, he might be the singer or the keyboard player—he gets fully outside himself. Doing that primes a person not to worry so much about how you play or what you play or how you're doing in someone else's estimation, because, in that moment, says Brock, "you're not even you."

To not be you is a great liberator of the imagination. This, of course, is central to why people still dive into old-fashioned role-play games like Dungeons and Dragons, or get lost in massively multiplayer online video games like Doom or World of Warcraft. Nick Fortugno, a video game designer and entrepreneur, got his start in two realms of role play: D&D as a kid; then as a young adult, live-action role-play games. The latter take place in public spaces amid an unsuspecting public. Think of "Tag" with a twist: all the players are characters in a narrative, and as they move among the throngs in New York's Grand Central Station or Greenwich Village, they are pursuing and evading one another, each with character-driven imperatives and a limited number of "influence" cards to play. The narrative might be a medieval mystery or a modern-day hunt for weapons of mass destruction.

For Fortugno, the power of such half-improvised role play is not only that it transports but also that "it teaches you that you can't have all the answers about a character or a situation." You have to stay open for the game to flow.

To imagine in this way—to conjure up the motivations and internalize the perspective of another—is one of the best ways to cultivate imagination. It may seem tautological to assert that you need imagination to have imagination, but just as it helps to have money to make money, so it is in this case. Like money, imagination compounds. Unlike money, imagination is endlessly renewable. Consider, for contrast, that although autistic children sometimes have savant-like artistic skills, they often struggle with pretend play, an imaginative endeavor that requires what psychologists call a theory of mind—an ability to attribute mental states to another person or to infer them from that person's behavior. (Or not even a person: the educator Richard Lewis tells, in *Living by Wonder,* of the ways he plays with child poets "to explore the 'interiority' of practically anything of interest to them: the dreaming of stones, of the sun, birds, frogs, and water.")

If there's a single word for this practice, it is *empathy*. Recently, neuroscientists in Sweden reported on a remarkable experiment in which they created, using video-rigged goggles, a "body-swapping" effect: you put on the special goggles, and now you see the world from someone else's vantage. You are virtually standing in that person's shoes. Your brain, relentless sense-making machine that it is, adapts readily to the new view. And then you're off. You inhabit this identity just as a video game player would an avatar. Where you were white before, now you can be black; where young, now elderly. Watch how people respond to you. If you take on the body of someone not just unlike you but someone you've always understood to be in opposition to you—the Arab to the Jew, say—then the transformation can be profound. Your capacity for empathy increases. You literally can feel someone's pain: the Swedish researchers found that their subjects cringe when the new body is threatened or prodded.

This is a testament not only to the plasticity of our brains but also to the power of a properly prodded imagination. But do we really need neuroscientists? Just think: each of us, being human, already comes preloaded with body-swapping goggles in our brain. Batteries included.

Make a Gap

Obscure part of the picture

H ere's how we are wired: If I take a word out of a sentence you may not notice it at first because brain uses what's available in context to patch any gap in content. *Your* brain, that is.

The mechanics of visual perception are wonderfully evolved to assist us in creating meaning wherever we look—and imposing it whether or not we want it. A simple example: Imagine four black Pac-Man shapes, positioned so that their open mouths form the illusion of a rectangle between them. Or four black discs, each with a curved slice missing, arrayed so that their missing curves face one another and form an illusory circle.

We see the shapes inside even though they are only implied. We can't not see the shapes. Yet there is not a real edge to be found. And just as our imaginations extrapolate from a few data points, they can also interpolate. That's why, for example, a cat behind a picket fence appears to be a whole cat, not a cat in slices. We assume the continuity of the cat in those gaps created by the pickets. We don't think twice about it. As the brain scientists V. S. Ramachandran and Diane Rogers-Ramachandran observe, "The richness of our individual experience is largely illusory; we actually 'see' very little and rely on educated guesswork to do the rest."

That guesswork is educated beyond estimation. The automatic gap-filling process—leaping instantaneously from the lowest subroutines of perception to the higher-order drive to synthesize a single coherent narrative—enables us not to get bogged down by the miraculous fact of having sensations. Think how long your day would seem if you had to stop each time you saw a cat and fence to determine whether a whole cat was there.

It's that same automatic gap-filling reflex of ours that skillful practitioners of imagination know how to play with. What is magic, after all, but the art of manipulating expectations of cause and effect? "You're asking people to put their reasoning brains to sleep," says the magician Eric Walton, "but they have to stay awake enough to know what's *supposed* to happen." Surprise comes only when the expected effect does not flow from the original cause. See a glass of water on the table, watch the magician cover it with a cloth, stand shocked when he pulls the cloth off and reveals no glass on the table! There are many tactics to create such surprise, as detailed in as Dariel Fitzkee's *Showmanship for Magicians* or Henning Nelms's *Magic and Showmanship*: misdirection, concealment, control of timing, angles, atmospherics. At the heart of the art, though, is the skill to create an intentional gap—in this case, what's happening when the cloth is on the glass?—and to invite us to fill that gap.

Edward Tufte, the guru of visual displays of information, observes that "techniques of disinformation design, *when reversed,* reinforce strategies of presentation used by good teachers." Where magicians seek to suppress context and prevent reflective analysis, teachers aim to set things in proper context and enable deep reflection. If you take apart an act of magic, you'll know how to put together an act of imagination. Great cultivators of imagination— great teachers—will deliberately obscure a crucial part of the story.

When the Tony-winning director Bartlett Sher brought to life his revival of Rodgers and Hammerstein's *South Pacific,* he employed a very conscious strategy of making the backdrops "analog," as he put it: painted with an old-fashioned, broad-brush feel that was suggestive rather than precise, an evocation of the islands rather than a reproduction. The problem with living today in a datascape of high-definition images that strive to be "sharper than reality" is that we become attuned to detail but passive: the higher the resolution of the picture, the lower *our* resolution to imagine its fullness.

Henning Nelms, in this regard, makes a key distinction between deception and conviction. A magic trick, whether by sleight of hand or by technology, may induce deception. What really matters, though, is earning the audience's conviction: "The playgoer never regards the events of a drama as real; he merely fails to disbelieve in them. This may seem like a weak basis for illusion but the result can be overwhelming. If the minds of audiences did not permit a suspension of disbelief, there would be no drama."

Sher wants an audience that is actively suspending disbelief, not deceived into believing that something not real is real. "I leave space and let the audience fill it in," he says. This is true of not only the staging of the set but, more important, of the way he directs his actors: Don't show all the emotions, he tells them; don't play the result. Hide something at the critical moment. "Chekhov," he reminds us, "exists more off the page than on." On every stage life presents, the magic of theater is to be found in the theater of magic.

Finish the Story

Make the ending open-ended

A variation on the "Make a Gap" theme is to "Finish the Story." As anyone who's ever read to children knows, denying the child the ending is a fantastic way to stimulate her imagination.

The weekly cartoon caption contest at the back of every issue of *The New Yorker* is another good example. Just as we can be primed by the start of a tale and then can exercise our imagination by being asked to finish it, so can we be stimulated by a predrawn comic setup awaiting a punchline.

Two men get off the elevator at work. One is holding a turkey under his arm. The other one says to him . . .

Chunk It

Show how small it all starts

Children and adults alike are sometimes frozen into inaction when told "The sky's the limit!" or "Imagine any kind of ___ you'd like!" The open-endedness can be paralyzing. In part that's because we are socialized early to embrace *what is* rather than *What if.* But it's also because imagining something novel can in fact be staggeringly hard. The blank page intimidates. The blue sky blinds. At times like that, it can help to break the process of imagining into chunks, to reveal each chunk as quite accessible, and thereby to demystify imagination.

Andrea Peterson is an elementary school music teacher in Granite Falls, Washington. She was named the National Teacher of the Year in 2007, and to watch her work— with learners of *any* age—is to see why. She has a knack for taking imagination down from the pedestal and making it something anyone can embrace.

Her fourth- and fifth-graders are creating a musical based on the book *The Phantom Tollbooth*. Their first task is to write a song about a city called Dictionopolis. "If you just say, 'Come up with a song,' that can be overwhelming," Peterson says. Instead, she segments the process and models it for them, segment by segment. "I try to show them how small you really start."

She begins with a free-writing exercise, which yields a line that might be a promising hook for a song: *We welcome you to our city*. Then she shows the kids how to use a thesaurus to find synonyms for the words in that line. *We hail you to our municipality. We greet you at our metropolis.* Then they play with musical hooks, and as she reads these lines aloud, she tells the kids that a funk beat has entered her head. Why? Who knows? But now there's a sound to experiment with. By this point, the students are saying to themselves, "I can do this." They're jumping in. They're conjuring up analogous approaches. For the next song, about numbers and the city of Digitopolis, they come up with equations that all yield the same result: the mathematical analogue to synonyms.

Great teachers know how to make play purposeful. At the MIT Media Lab, the celebrated composer Tod Machover has invented high-tech, low-prep ways of making music. His Hyperscore software program allows anyone to compose music by manipulating blobs and spikes of color on the screen. No knowledge of musical notation or theory is required. His Hyperinstruments look like toys—squishy balls and bright bugs—but they are programmed to take simple human movements and convert them into harmonious sound and rhythm. All these tools demolish barriers to entry into the realm of music.

Machover has been mentored by legends as diverse as the composer Elliott Carter and the artificial intelligence pioneer Marvin Minsky. He has collaborated with Yo-Yo Ma and Prince. But when asked who has done the most to unlock his capacity for imagination, he doesn't hesitate. It's Mom. When Machover was a toddler, he and a group of other three- and four-year-olds would take piano lessons from his mother, a Juilliard-trained pianist and a true master of imagination. She created a "floor staff" to teach the children about notes. It was a big plastic mat with the five lines of a musical staff. She would throw bean bags onto the mat and sing the notes they landed on. She would call out a note and invite the children to jump on it. She would end each lesson with five minutes of exploration: each child was asked to find an object in the house that had a nice sound to it and bring it back to the circle. Which one was loudest? Which one softest? What happened if you banged two objects together? What happened if you struck one while speaking a word?

Machover learned from his mother that "music is not something dead people wrote for you to interpret; it's a way of telling a story, with your body." He learned as well that the best way to teach such storytelling is to break it down playfully. To make the first principles and basic elements accessible. To hint at what could happen beyond this step and the next.

Andrea Peterson was described earlier as having a knack for such work—but maybe that's not the best word, because "knack" sounds like "gift," which sounds like "bestowed by the gods." In fact, what she has is a *habit*: a skill she has intentionally developed and reinforced. "In my family," she says, "my brother, a music producer and composer, has the real musical gift," she says. "I'm not one of those truly gifted people—and that's helped with my success as a teacher. I can verbalize things and explain them because I had to figure them out for myself."

To an outsider, the work of conjuring a song from thin air seems to happen in a black box. Peterson and Machover open the black box. Peterson shows her students that inside is not magic but method. "I didn't start with any specific inspiration," she says. "I started with a thesaurus." Machover, for all his musical pedigree, started with pots and pans. His students start with blobs and bugs. From there, they figure out what's possible. Segmenting an act of imagination into smaller, graspable acts keeps learners motivated. It collapses the distance from blank slate to idea, then from idea to creation. It doesn't matter who we are or where the classroom is. Each little success leads to a greater one, and soon, our confidence compounded, we learn we have it within us to compose songs—and even more important, to imagine them.

practice 14

Don't Blink

*Snap in slow motion; see how you get
primed for decision*

O ne lesson that so many of us drew from *Blink,* Malcolm Gladwell's wide-ranging survey of intuition and "the power of thinking without thinking," is that our snap judgments of people or situations, based on thin slices of evidence, are often more accurate than deeply considered analyses.

This is absolutely true—except when it isn't. And when it isn't, it can be very dangerous.

The work of cultivating imagination is, in some respects, the work of deferring the blink—keeping eyes pried open—and suspending the process of judgment formation. As Gladwell himself concludes, the dark side of trusting snap judgments is falling prey to harmful stereotypes and rationalizing them. The New York City policemen who shot African immigrant Amadou Diallo dozens of times made a snap judgment about black men. For those officers, there was a tight implicit association between blackness and danger that under stress became fatally explicit. In that moment, it seemed they literally could not imagine a different association.

Thinking without thinking, in short, is only as good as the underlying nonthinking—that is, how wide a pool of associations we unwittingly draw from. The practice this suggests is twofold: in the first place, to name our snap judgments; and in the second, to prime ourselves for other kinds of judgments.

Naming is a simple thing but it has great power. By articulating our usually unstated and even unconscious associations, we create distance from them. We can hold them like an object, regarding every linkage and asking where it came from. We can then train ourselves to break the negative associations or at least to contemplate alongside them a set of neutral or positive ones.

And this is where it matters how we prime ourselves. Psychologists describe both perceptual and conceptual priming: the former, where reacting to a visual stimulus—say, a serpent—primes you to respond similarly when you see a similar stimulus, such as a hose; the latter, where thinking of one concept (serpent) makes you prone to talk about an adjacent one (Eden). Priming works because our minds are much more top-down than we realize: they are always struggling to make orderly stories out of the filaments and flotsam of experience. Our minds are ruthless filters, selecting and discarding with purpose. To foster imagination is, in good measure, to change our meaning-filters from time to time.

V. S. Ramachandran puts it well: "It is almost as though we are all hallucinating all the time," he writes, "and what we call object perception merely involves *selecting* the one hallucination that matches the current sensory input, however fragmentary. Vision, in short, is controlled hallucination." Blink, then, if you must. But do so with a willingness to have a *new* hallucination—a black man not as a predator, but as a president—when your eyes reintroduce you to the world.

Cloud
Appreciation

Search out ambiguity and sit with it

LUCY: Aren't the clouds beautiful? They look like big balls of cotton. I could just lie here all day and watch them drift by. If you use your imagination, you can see lots of things in the clouds' formations. What do you think you see, Linus?

LINUS: Well, those clouds up there look to me like the map of the British Honduras on the Caribbean. [points up] That cloud up there looks a little like the profile of Thomas Eakins, the famous painter and sculptor. And that group of clouds over there . . . [points] . . . gives me the impression of the Stoning of Stephen. I can see the Apostle Paul standing there to one side.

LUCY: Uh huh. That's very good. What do you see in the clouds, Charlie Brown?

*CHARLIE BROWN: Well . . . I was going to say I
saw a duckie and a horsie, but I changed my mind.*

Among the many life lessons that Charlie Brown and his
gang have taught us is the art of using the clouds as a
Rorschach test. Look up at the sky. What do you see?
Duckies and horsies? Cannon fire? A boy kicking a
football?

Popular volumes on creativity and imagination always
extol the virtues of "blue-sky thinking." But the Cloud
Appreciation Society, based in Somerton, England, issued
a founding manifesto that includes this commitment:
"We pledge to fight 'blue-sky thinking' wherever we find
it. Life would be dull if we had to look up at cloudless
monotony day after day." So it would. The Society has
published a little volume called *Hot Pink Flying Saucers*
that consists of photographs of all kinds of clouds, and
what they can be interpreted to be. Salvador Dali's face.
The Michelin Man robbing a bank. A hot pink flying
saucer.

It's a delightful book, and its spirit is to be applauded and
propagated. Even better, though, would be a book of such
photos without the captions, or with blank lines for
alternate captions. As with a Rorschach inkblot, the
power of the image of a cloud is in its open-endedness.
What do you think it looks like?

The conceptual paradigm shifts that Thomas Kuhn wrote about in *The Structure of Scientific Revolutions* are, on some basic level, akin to changes in visual gestalt: "The marks on paper that were first seen as a bird," he noted, "are now seen as an antelope, or vice versa." The question, then, is how to catalyze such reinterpretations of gestalt. And a good part of the answer is to expose ourselves as much as possible to clouds or inkblots or anything that can be interpreted any number of ways. In recent decades Rorschach tests have been discredited as reliable markers of a person's psychological state. But that doesn't mean they need to be discredited as vitamins for the imagination.

The artist and musician Brian Eno several decades ago created a deck of cards called "Oblique Strategies" (the limited edition decks are now collector's items; fortunately they now exist virtually as a delightful iTunes app). Each of the over one hundred cards contains what Eno calls "a worthwhile dilemma"—a concise, cryptic prompt like "What mistake did you make last time?" or "Remember quiet evenings" or "Ask people to work against their better judgment" or "Use filters" or "Make what's perfect more human." Like horoscopes, they are meant to give direction; even more than horoscopes, they are precise in their vagueness and they hit you where you least expect it—because that combination of specificity and randomness speeds you down pathways of association.

If you have a dilemma, then, a ready way to make it worthwhile is to convert it into a form that is subject to widely varying interpretations. Share with your team only a keyhole's worth of the problem—a strange, ambiguous slice—and let them extrapolate or imagine what's beyond the keyhole. Watch how they see: it will reveal much about what to do. Or turn over an Oblique Strategy card, and you just might get this one: "Change ambiguities to specifics." That's what it means to spark imagination.

Spotlight Off, Lantern On

Trade sharp focus for full-field awareness

"B abies are more conscious than we are."

So declares Alison Gopnik, the Berkeley developmental psychologist and early childhood expert. What she means is this: as nonbabies, we have vivid consciousness of what we're focused on but we inhibit awareness of the rest. Indeed, this is what it means cognitively to move beyond babyhood. We focus on some things, we ignore others. We chunk things up into bigger and bigger concepts so that at the first indication of a chunk we know where to file the sensation. Rather rapidly, what William James called the "bloomin' buzzin' confusion" recedes and we learn to perceive with the jaded predictability of experience. Babies, by contrast, attend to everything at once. They may be terribly confused by their inability to prioritize, to discern borders and units of mass or sound or color. But there's no question that their virgin senses are taking it all in. The difference between these kinds of consciousness, as Gopnik frames it, is the difference between the spotlight and the lantern. And in her view, adults would do well to rediscover the lantern.

It takes some effort to rewind to that infantile state of undiscriminating awareness. You have no shortcuts from percept to concept. But without shortcuts, you end up with *more* consciousness, not less. Think of being in a foreign country where everything is unintelligible to you: much more than at home, you are acutely aware of your surroundings and alert to meaning at every turn. And every turn is a wrong turn, until it's not. You have not only permission but obligation to question how everything hangs together.

How can we uncorrect our vision on demand? In yoga, a great instructor knows just the moment—as her students strain to hold a pose, muscles aching and minds racing— to drop a simple transformative command: "Soften your gaze." What does that mean? Partly it means a relaxation of the muscles of the face and the eyes. More, it means loosening the grip of the sense-making intellect and yielding to a more limbic form of awareness. Our object-recognizing prefrontal cortex, as powerful and relentless as a magnet, yearns to pull together stray components (green, shiny, clumped) into a unified thing (bunch of apples). To soften the gaze is to drape that magnet in heavy cloth. Now watch as those loose elements float, join in unlikely combination, detach. Are they apples, candles, cans?

When we see the world with the lantern instead of the spotlight, what we see is *how* to see. In Jonah Lehrer's wonderful *Proust Was a Neuroscientist* we learn that Paul Cézanne honed a style in which chunks and swaths of color and shape are arrayed to suggest mountains and lakes and fruit—but only to suggest. The postimpressionist style he pioneered does not treat a painting as a photographic representation. But it captures in high fidelity what goes on in our brains when our eyes first encounter a scene.

"As Cézanne understood," writes Lehrer, "seeing is imagining." Every millisecond, through the alchemy of memory and imagination, we transform blurs into forms we know and can understand. Cézanne aimed to rewind our vision to that moment before the blur sharpens up—and to remind us, by beautiful metaphor, that we are *always* forcing forms top-down onto those blurs. He captures in his paintings that stage of perception before sensory inputs have flowed into the preformed molds of our higher minds. He softens our gaze. *Our* job, lanterns on, is to search out new forms.

Play Telephone

Engage in meaning-laundering

W hen children play telephone, they are amused by the degradation of the message as it's passed along the circle. But what if generating such low-fidelity transmission were the *point* of the game?

David Herskovits, working from the cramped upstairs offices of his Target Margin Theater in Brooklyn, has become celebrated for arrestingly offbeat adaptations of classics. When Herskovits prepares the actors in his company for a new production, he sometimes has them play an advanced and somewhat twisted form of telephone. He gives two actors a speech, from a classic like Aristophanes' *The Frogs*. He says to them, "You have two minutes to learn it—go!" Then that pair has to pass the speech on to another pair of actors. This next pair has thirty seconds to memorize what they've just heard and recite it to another pair. The next pair in turn gives their version of the speech to a secretary, who's recording it furiously with pen and paper and then must deliver the transcription. And on and on.

"What you get," Herskovits says with devious glee, "is a layered devouring, a digestion and regurgitation of the play." This process of iterative translation is powerful because while it bastardizes the surface it purifies the core. What seems like contamination of the text as it's passed from one mouth to another is in fact an exquisite form of laundering. At the end of the chain Herskovits throws out most of the mutated speech but what remains is a set of truly useful nuggets that capture the essence of the consumed scene. And *that's* what gets performed. It's translation reframed: faithfulness not to the lyrics but to the music. "There's the words on the page," says Herskovits, "and there's the play. They're not necessarily the same."

The game reveals the creative audacity inherent in any act of translation. It seems like a simple thing to translate a concept from one language to another. A cat is *chat* in French or *mao* in Mandarin or *koshka* in Russian. But string together a few concepts—put the objects out of isolation and in relation to one another—and now you have a choice to make. Consider a haiku of rustic reminiscence. What matters more in the translation—the integrity of the 5/7/5 syllabic scheme or the integrity of the poem's emotional valence? What about the visual symbolism of the original Japanese ideographs?

What, when you get right down to it, is a syllable?

To translate is to invoke an aesthetic allegiance, to be forced to declare a preferred pathway (or digestive tract) for interpreting and expressing ideas. It is to make a choice about which patterns matter. 5/7/5 is a pattern. So is pastoral nostalgia. So is the idea of a poem. So is the poet. So are you. So is how you respond to poems. When we engage in any act of translation, let alone Target Margin's iterative translation, we are breaking things down to their essential patterns of meaning, value, behavior, quality, interrelationship. We get to see them side by side. And this breaking down, this roughing up and cracking open of the smooth surfaces of what we call reality, allows shafts of imagination to shine through. Now, having knocked one pattern off the pedestal of inviolability, we can contemplate remaking and refitting *all* the patterns in our lives. They are but symbols to manipulate, meanings to negotiate.

Imagine, if you will, playing the Herskovits game with your organization's latest strategy memo or a joint communiqué between heads of state or your annual performance review or your therapist's take on how you interact with your parents or children. What essences would remain? What surprises would emerge? What possibilities would arise?

The telephone is ringing.

Help Out a Boobonian

Make every task a quest

A group of Boobonians have been kicked off their home planet and materialize in a universe where only Spanish is spoken. Your challenge is to help these aliens learn it—and quickly, so that they can survive. Every week they transmit to you an artifact from their new universe: a map, calendar, a weather report, a diagram of the body. You've got to help them make sense of these artifacts in their new tongue. Conveniently, you can converse with them using an interstellar version of Skype.

Got that?

If you're one of Katie Salen's students, you got it and you're running with it. Salen, who teaches at Parsons The New School for Design, is one of the country's foremost experts on game design. Her 2004 book, *Rules of Play*, is an encyclopedic review of the grammar and heuristics of every form of game one can imagine, from spin the bottle to backgammon to Centipede to SimCity and hundreds of points between. She herself is an omnivorous player of games, from intense online games to Division I volleyball during her college years. And her latest endeavor is launching a pioneering public school, grades 6–12, based on the principles of video gaming.

Some adults may at this point be gasping in horror, but such a school does not represent the ultimate debasement of education. On the contrary, it represents a great hope. For the central gaming principle at work in Salen's school is this: *create a need to know.* The Boobonian exercise, which Salen developed for a sixth-grade Spanish class, illustrates this well. By designing such challenge-based learning modules, particularly one where the students have to shepherd helpless aliens, Salen has created stakes where none had existed before. And that generates motivation. Learning Spanish now matters to the kids in her class—not because they have to teach it to a bunch of aliens but because they *get* to teach it.

A second principle borrowed from gaming and activated by the Boobonians is to *create a need to share.* All the students realize that by collaborating they will accomplish their goal more quickly. The advantages of sharing are in fact embedded in the design the exercise. And the sharing activates a third principle of questing: *spark learning across networks.* When her students go on "data expeditions" to find the Spanish phrases and referents they need, they cross boundaries. And when, in a related exercise, Salen asks the kids to conduct ethnographies of the spaces they move in, they chart with indiscriminate curiosity and attention to detail the library, Grandma's apartment, the World of Warcraft, fan-fiction Web sites. As they negotiate and translate their way across these disparate domains, the children are becoming literate not only in Spanish or English but also in the syntax of learning.

Quests have rules and rituals and limits. Quests require embodying the work. They demand deep noticing and pattern recognition. They reward reflection. What John Seely Brown calls "the questing disposition" has to be the heart of any kind of imaginative education. Designing for this disposition is a variation on the practice of deploying myth and narrative. It's more, though: it's inventing an entire ecosystem in which the quest—and the quester's imagination—can emerge playfully and organically and in the context of a community.

The schools in Lincoln Center Institute's orbit follow this approach, as does any school that uses project-based learning and fosters a culture of inquiry. Learning to discover honors the spirit of a quest; learning to repeat a result does not.

In a computer program like a flight simulator, points out Seely Brown, the player's imagination is used sparingly and only to draw a tight and rather literal analogy between the simulation and the experience it apes. But in the questing environment of massively multiplayer online games like World of Warcraft or Ultima Online, the player's imagination is activated fully because she is simultaneously in and out of role, reacting to stimuli both as the person she is in the physical world and as the character she is in the virtual. Sometimes those converge, sometimes they diverge. Managing that tension both feeds and draws on the imagination. This is the realm not of analogy but of metaphor. You are not *like* a hero; you *are* the hero. So you play with commitment.

The problem is that too much of formal education—for adults and children alike—is run like a flight simulator, where a premium is placed on replication of a result rather than discovery of a role. Replication may be more amenable to measurement, but discovery is better preparation for how to *be*. The difference is the difference between playback and play, between copying and creating. As any good Boobonian could tell you, the latter is the point of true learning. So enlist your comrades and go on a quest. For a quest worth having.

Teach Nonzero Math

Expand the pie before dividing it

I t's often said, and it seems rather true, that life is a negotiation. It's therefore rather remarkable how deep a rut most people stay in when it comes to the art of negotiating. Whether the setting is the dinner table at dessert time or the treaty table in wartime, we learn to conceptualize bargaining as a zero-sum battle. If you win, I lose. But as Roger Fisher and William Ury of the Harvard Negotiation Project wrote in their classic guide *Getting to Yes,* "Skill at inventing options is one of the most useful assets a negotiator can have." The imaginative negotiator "expands the pie before dividing it."

Getting to Yes devotes a core section to inventing options for mutual gain. As they see it, there are four impediments to the generation of nonzero outcomes: premature criticism of a novel approach, fixation on a single result, assumption of a fixed pie, and thinking that "solving their problem is their problem." Each of these is a failure of imagination. And Fisher and Ury propose four remedies: first, to separate inventing from deciding, thus suspending negative judgment; second, to multiply possible outcomes by creating "weaker" versions of an ideal deal or varying the scope of the deal; third, to seek out differences that can dovetail; and fourth, to find ways to address preemptively the other side's interests.

All these remedies require the kind of self-awareness and empathy, and the ability to reframe frames, that are critical to a healthy imagination. Of them, the third is perhaps the most interesting. Fisher and Ury describe a scene where two children are arguing over who gets an orange. They finally decide to split it in half, only to realize later that one wanted to eat the fruit while the other really wanted the peel for baking. Had they fully explored their differing interests they might have seen that those differences could have given rise to a better agreement. "This is genuinely startling if you think about it," write Fisher and Ury. "People generally assume that differences between two parties create the problem. Yet differences can also lead to a solution."

A common clever way to express the idea of nonzero-sum outcomes is to say that you want to make $1+1 = 3$. That, of course, is a nice trick. In the context of negotiations, though, where so often the function is not addition but division, perhaps a more apt formula would be this: $1 \div 2 = 2$. *That's* new math. And to teach and model it is to open more widely the scope of imagination.

Microexperiment

Test your hunches playfully

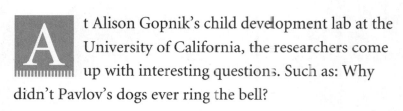

At Alison Gopnik's child development lab at the University of California, the researchers come up with interesting questions. Such as: Why didn't Pavlov's dogs ever ring the bell?

Stop and think about that for a moment. When Ivan Pavlov rang a bell at feeding time, the dogs in his experiments learned to associate the bell with the food. Pretty soon, the bell alone, and not the presence of any food, was enough to get the dogs salivating. But the question that struck Gopnik was simple. Why didn't those dogs ever make an imaginative leap from association to causation? Why didn't they test whether tapping a bell with a paw might *cause* food to appear?

The question itself has profound implications for imagination and the study of causation, which we'll get to in the next practice. What's interesting here is how Gopnik's team went about investigating it. They had a question, maybe a guess as to the answer, and a desire to see how it would be answered with kids instead of dogs. Rather than erecting the scaffolding for a full-on double-blind scientific study, they simply piloted. They ran dozens of little pre-experiments, often with just two or three kids. They brainstormed variations on Pavlov: get a machine with a beeper and a marble; when the marble comes out, the machine beeps. Will a preschooler test whether pressing the beeper *makes* the marble come out?

This is something more strategic than throwing stuff at the wall to see what sticks; it's throwing stuff *of a certain kind* at the wall. The architect and playground designer David Rockwell runs his firm, the Rockwell Group, this way. He describes the controlled chaos of his studio as a "three-dimensional habitable collage." It's filled with stray objects and sketches and toys from random places. And whenever a client comes in with a mission, the team clears a space amidst the messiness for rapid prototyping. Quick, provisional portable solutions emerge from the chatter and tinkering. That's true whether the mission is something somber like the post-9/11 World Trade Center viewing platform, or something whimsical like theater spaces for Cirque du Soleil.

Induction is the way of most cognition. We collect data points and try to discern whether patterns emerge.

Deduction is the way of geniuses like Einstein: they postulate a pattern from the start and work backward to prove it. *Targeted* induction of the kind Gopnik and Rockwell and their teams practice lies somewhere in between. They start with neither a postulate nor a blank slate but with a clear question. Why didn't Pavlov's dogs ring the bell? How does one strike a balance between dignity and accessibility at Ground Zero? And with the question as a fixed point, a North Star, they go forth and explore.

Getting the question right is essential, and it's what makes this kind of play more serious than the pretend play of the children in Gopnik's studies or Rockwell's playgrounds. The question about Pavlov's dogs entered Gopnik's mind only after years of looking at, looking away from, and looking back at the data of her field. Then she turned to adjacent fields. The more deeply she studied causation— from the vantage points of psychology, morality, artificial intelligence, history, literature—the more clearly her question emerged.

So how do you find great questions? Consume, digest, ask, play. And in a hundred little experiments, repeat.

Rewrite History

Turn "what would've been" into "what could be"

"The quaint conceit of imagining what would have happened if some important or unimportant event had settled itself differently has become so fashionable that I am encouraged to enter upon an absurd speculation. What would have happened if Lee had not won the Battle of Gettysburg?"

These are the opening lines of a wickedly imaginative essay Winston Churchill published in 1930. In it, Churchill writes *as if Lee had won* and he proceeds, in earnest, to unfurl a chain of suppositions about how the world would have evolved had Lee lost. The Civil War would have ended sooner, Churchill surmises; America would not have split into two weakened nations; the ensuing three-nation alliance with England would not have emerged; England, isolated, would not have been able to thwart the ambitions of the continental powers like Germany in 1914; and the result would have been a world war.

Churchill's agenda at the time was to advocate for an Anglo-American alliance that could help avert a second world war in Europe. But instead of making the argument straight, he tells a tortuous history and bends the minds of his readers—and in the process, he awakens us to the contingency and fragility of what we, in hindsight, perceive to have been the inevitable "march" of historical forces. Even today, when we know how things turned out for Churchill and the English-speaking peoples, his thought experiment thrills.

The word for such thoughts is *counterfactual*—asking what would have been the case if some antecedent had been true. Or to put it another way: What would be the *then* if you had another *if*?

To a professional historian, counterfactuals are mere "fictional questions" that might be illuminating but can't be taken seriously. But to someone like Churchill, who aimed not so much to report on the world as to transform it, counterfactuals are powerful tools. They make visible and explicit our assumptions and unspoken wishes and visions. What kind of world do we want? What unrealized possibilities do we seek? How do we build toward them?

As counterfactuals go, "What if Lee had lost" is rather sophisticated. But the counterfactual habit is as basic as thinking itself. Once we as toddlers begin to comprehend cause and effect, we begin to make a causal map of the world. We ask, *What if*? What if I push this ball? What if I cover my eyes? What if I touch this bright thing? As a result of all this testing, says Alison Gopnik, we learn to imagine. "The same thing that helps us understand the world allows us, for free, to have imagination. You couldn't have one without the other."

Then it's a short leap from causation to counterfactuals. We simply aim the light of *What if* behind us. The psychologist Paul Harris, who has documented the richly textured nature of children's play, finds it rife with counterfactuals. Harris ran an experiment in which two- and three-year-olds watch as two toy horses are made to gallop across a table. One gallops to the very edge, while the other stops well short. When asked which horse *almost* fell off, the children could answer correctly. Even at this age they could discern and express an unrealized possibility, and identify the element that determined or averted an outcome.

Along the way, though, the counterfactual muscle of our minds falls into disuse. As we grow older, we inhibit wide-open exploration. We stop rearranging the what-ifs and the if-thens, and when we use the counterfactual muscle at all we do so in service of work, of the practical.

The first thing we can do to rebuild that muscle is simply play more: give ourselves time each day when we forge together counterfactual chains just for the fun of it. "What kids have and what adults need," observes Gopnik, "is counterfactuals detached from goals." Pay attention to the world—its physical laws, its mores and politics, its beauty and squalor—and ask yourself and others: How would things be different now if something earlier had been different? What other possible worlds would be unspooled from such a question?

But, as Harris warns, the quality of our counterfactuals is inherently limited by the quality of the antecedents we choose. For instance, he reports, when children study a pendulum and try to determine the causes of its oscillation, they can entertain counterfactuals with each of the variables at hand: length of the string, force of the push, weight of the pendulum. What they overlook is gravity. The rate of oscillation would be slower on the moon, for instance, but they rarely consider that. Being on Earth is the most important overlooked variable.

So the second thing we can do is identify our own blind spots for possible antecedents. What's the equivalent of being on Earth, the thing we take for granted? Why, indeed, should we take *anything* for granted? Our climate, our markets, our castes, our preferences, our indulgences, our ethics?

Churchill's first point in the Lee essay was historical: at any moment, things could have gone differently. His second point was philosophical: at any moment, things can *still* go differently. In human affairs, as in physics, there is an uncertainty principle. Everything is indeterminate, and *interdependently* indeterminate. Our acts change other people's acts and thus change the world. If we practice teasing apart the web of causation that brought us what we have, we can more ably bring into being what we want.

We just need more time with Churchill, or children, to appreciate that power.

Design for the Hallway

Let informal spaces thrive

E very summer, on an idyllic island near Vancouver, British Columbia, a group of successful and idealistic aging ex-hippies gathers at a retreat center called Hollyhock. The Summer Invitational, as the gathering is called, is a weeklong form of intellectual and spiritual camp. There are guest speakers and workshops on leadership and social change, semispontaneous Open Space sessions on creativity and healing, organic vegetarian feasts, group song and dance experiences. Though the conference is not large, it requires a great deal of planning and preparation. But the Hollyhock Summer Invitational runs ultimately on a principle stated by Rick Ingrasci, one of its organizers: "The best stuff at a conference usually happens in the hallway, so we've tried to create a conference that's *all hallway!*"

How do you do that? The magic of in-between-session chats and serendipitous epiphanies at the watercooler— the stuff you can't get in the "regular" sessions—is elusive. It depends on the very structure that it resists. For if you actually eliminate all the sessions at a conference, no form remains and therefore no interstices. An office that's all watercooler and no desks can be as imagination draining as an office that's the reverse. Affordances make themselves known only in the presence of constraints. So designing for the hallway is a subtle art.

In the corridors of the National Security Agency, which are about as distant spiritually as geographically from Hollyhock, Eric Haseltine tried to practice that art. When Haseltine, a technology futurist and former Disney Imagineer, was hired as the chief technology officer of the post-9/11 NSA, it seemed an inspired mismatch. Haseltine was brought in to be a catalyst—to spark chemical reactions—and he did just that, stirring up the culture of the notoriously secretive code-cracking agency. He didn't last long. But he knew he wouldn't, and while he was there, he was strategic about how he wanted to go about catalyzing.

Haseltine tells a story passed down among Imagineers about how in the early years of Disneyland the workers kept patching up grass and flowers that guests stepped on. Walt Disney, noticing this, told the workers that instead of trying to force the guests to follow a pre-paved path, they should watch where the guests walk and pave there. "You're pretty much hosed if you're trying to make people change in a large bureaucracy," Haseltine says. So rather than try to impose top-down a new approach to the spy business, Haseltine made like Disney: he noticed how people *naturally* wanted to move, and built around it.

He approached the cultivation of imagination as a form of covert action. He found the best scientists in the agency and watched what they naturally wanted to do, which was to trade ideas. He created a Fellows program, inviting them to have informal under-the-radar conversations. He ran meetings with scientists and analysts where, as he puts it, he could "intentionally plan accidents." And when interesting ideas arose, such as creating a Wikipedia of top-secret content for the intelligence community, he provided cover for those ideas to develop. A meeting on innovation was the last place where innovation happened. "The informal always beats the formal," Haseltine insists.

So it is at Hollyhock. The breaks, not the sessions, are where palpable connections often are formed among these earnest changemakers. As the guests walk the lush gardens and the sheltering woods, they talk, share, and link up emerging strands of idea-DNA. But this happens because the formal sessions are where the primordial soup first gets stirred. There is no informal *without* the formal. What helped Haseltine tolerate the frustrations of large agency life was the knowledge that the bureaucracy was the grain against which he could cut; that without it, he was sculpting air.

Says Haseltine, "You can't *stop* imagination; it's there. Just by the law of averages, any group of people will have it." His task, as he saw it, was to create a place where the imagination of individuals in the agency could flow, where even from a trickle it could carve a channel that could deepen and widen and, eventually, like the Grand Canyon, become more notable for the open space it cleared out than for the edifice that contained it.

Whatever your arena, then, be it purpose finding or intelligence gathering, there's no need to rail against the existence of silos, walls, hives. Just nurture the spaces between: that's where the true secrets of imagination are to be found.

Routinize Randomness

Regularly rinse out expectations

I t's late 2008, and there's a game going around Facebook called "What's on Page 56?" Here are the rules:

- Grab the book nearest you. Right now.

- Turn to page 56.

- Find the fifth sentence.

- Post that sentence along with these instructions.

- Don't dig for your favorite book, the coolest, the most intellectual. Use the CLOSEST.

And that's it. You don't have to know how Facebook works at all to try the game (although part of the fun of it on a social networking site is sharing your findings with others). All you have to do is be willing to follow this routine. What emerges is totally random. Sometimes that fifth sentence is completely pertinent to your life at this very minute. Sometimes it falls flat. Other times, the meaning of the sentence sinks in only gradually. Every time, it makes you think. It opens up a sense of interconnectedness, because it awakens your desire to *find* interconnectedness. And then it makes you wonder whether that desire might be obscuring—impeding— something else, an even deeper awareness.

Once, years ago, director David Herskovits was rehearsing a play when a cat outside the theater began meowing loudly. He liked the sound of it. His crew recorded the cat, edited the tape, and inserted meows at random points in the performance. There was no answer to the inevitable question from audiences: *Why the cats?* "If you can just explain it with a simple answer," says Herskovits, "then who cares?" So he began in other productions to harness random happenings. During an O'Neill production, he was frustrated by the flatness of a scene. To shake things up, he directed someone offstage to bang a piece of wood at a critical moment in the dialogue. The fact that the line was now inaudible made the audience lean in, wonder. *What did he say? What could have been said?* Herskovits had planned for surprise, and it freed up the scene.

Planning for surprise is not a method; it's a mindset. In some forms of Zen Buddhist teaching, the master will without warning strike the pupil with a stick. Not because there was a "wrong" answer or an offending statement. Just because. To the student who gets thwacked in the middle of a catechism, it seems painfully arbitrary. "Is this stick real or not real?" asks the master. If the student says "Real," he is struck; if he says "Not real," he is struck. Then perhaps the master will blurt out something completely nonsensical: "Three times three is nine!" To an observer, it is theater of the absurd. But the master is wielding the Zen stick with intention: to snap the student out of his insatiable desire to bifurcate self from surroundings. To keep the student's mind from inventing *expectations*.

Expectations are one of the great enemies of imagination. Whether the thing we expect is wanted or unwanted, it creates a swell of psychic sound that drowns out everything else. This is not "woo-woo" stuff. Businesses have expectations: aren't public companies punished or rewarded every quarter depending on whether they "met expected earnings per share"? Politicians have them: isn't the game of the presidential debate not to beat the opponent but to "beat the expectations of conventional wisdom"? Families have them: don't so many children chart courses just to meet or reject their parents' expectations?

Randomness is disorienting because it scrambles the sequence of expectation. We don't know what should come next. *What could have been said?* When that happens, our minds open. Maybe there's a more meaningful way to value a company. Maybe there is a more substantive way to evaluate a debate. Maybe there is a more orthogonal way to be the child of your parents. Disorientation is good for the imagination.

So embrace the randomness when it comes. And make a habit—a routine, even—of making some randomness of your own. Turn to page 56. *Thwack!* Or don't.

Ride the z-axis

*Find elemental forms, then play
with scale*

F riedrich Wilhelm Froebel is not a household name in America, but he should be. Froebel is the German educator who, in 1840, created the world's first kindergarten. At the heart of his vision was what he called "the gifts": a set of objects that, introduced in sequence, would reveal to children the essential forms of nature and suggest the interplay of limitless combinations.

The gifts are blocks, rings, parquetry tiles, strings, cylinders, balls, sticks, cubes, and clay They are, as Norman Brosterman writes in *Inventing Kindergarten*, an almost perfectly designed system for releasing the imagination. They "progressed from solid, to plane, to line, to point, and then reversed to arrive back in three dimensions," opening the mind like a bellows. Frank Lloyd Wright spent many childhood days with Froebel's gifts, and the results are plainly visible in his buildings. Paul Klee learned to play with lines by playing with the gifts. Buckminster Fuller's sense of shape and space was awakened by the gifts.

Fast-forward a century, to Madison Avenue. Alex Osborn is not a household name, but he should be. Osborn is the advertising guru and cofounder of BBDO who, in 1948, invented the brainstorm. Literally. In his book *Your Creative Power,* he not only coined the term (likening it to storming the fortress of blocked thinking), but he also laid out a detailed method for idea generation that has spread like few memes in modern history.

In Osborn's view, there are two parts to a good brainstorm: deferment of judgmental thinking, and raw quantity. When there are no stupid ideas, there are lots of ideas, and when there are lots of ideas, there are lots of good ideas. Although it's often true that quantity begets quality, it's also true that quality has more than one dimension. Many groups, when they brainstorm, think horizontally: they aim to populate an empty space with ideas. The result can be sprawl. Osborn knew that thinking vertically is a powerful way to concentrate the benefits of brainstorming. In ideation, as in urban planning, density creates connections.

Among Osborn's vertical practices was the instruction to "maxify and minify." Blowing up something to the nth degree, making it preposterously overstated, is a useful way to play with an idea or an object. Ask: How could it be expanded, exaggerated? How does that distortion illuminate possibilities or limitations? In the same spirit, miniaturizing a thing or simply reducing it in magnitude can also reveal its hidden aspects or properties. How could we use less of it or condense it or shrink one element of it? How does that change how we see the *it*?

What this practice amounts to is zooming up and down a z-axis instead of just roaming around the x and y. It's what David McConville's GeoDome enables people to do when he takes them through each power of ten from Earth to cosmos. And it's what the photographer Chris Jordan does in his breathtaking images of the mass consumption and waste of modern society.

Jordan, a onetime lawyer who succumbed to his love of photography, made his name with pictures of trash. For his first series of works, *Intolerable Beauty*, he wandered junkyards and took wall-sized digital photos of the refuse he found: oil drums, crushed cars, abandoned computers, discarded cell phones, shredded steel. All in staggeringly large piles and stacks. These gorgeous images, manscapes of industrial shame, awakened the conscience.

His next series, *Running the Numbers*, awakened the imagination. Here, Jordan didn't take things as he found them; he played with them. He started with an image of, for instance, a dozen forty-two-gallon barrels of crude oil. Next, he photoshopped the starter image many times over, assembling the copies meticulously—obsessively—into concentric circles of seemingly infinite regress.

The result is a stunning composite image of precisely 28,000 barrels—also known as two minutes of American oil consumption. In another image, 32,000 naked Barbie dolls are arrayed to make a sixty-by-eighty-inch montage of Barbie's breasts—32,000 being the number of elective breast augmentation surgeries performed monthly in the United States in 2006. In another, we see a brilliant galaxy. Look more closely, and you notice that it consists of 320,000 light bulbs—the number of kilowatt-hours wasted every minute by inefficient residential electricity usage.

By telling us with his Froebelesque patterns that one consolidated image equals one unit of consumption, Jordan is at once maxifying and minifying. Each image he creates can be broken down into its constituent parts or it can be rolled up, recursively, into even more massive patterns of consumption. Up and down the z-axis we go. As we contemplate these images of images of images, we begin to realize that if we can play with scale this way to visualize consumption, we can surely do so to visualize—and then effect—conservation.

But something more than the political point sinks in. We begin to wonder what else in our experience might be amenable to such depictions. Our treatment of neighbors? The effects of our management style? The time we spend helping others? We begin to wonder how else we might manipulate and arrange the components of our lives. Take a snapshot of yourself at work, at home, at play. Zoom. Add, multiply, divide, invert, substitute, recombine. What meta-image emerges? What montage suggests itself? To be able to see oneself and one's world this way is truly a gift: a gift we've all been given.

Challenge Your Challenges

Find better problems

T here's nothing like a challenge to stir the imagination.

Charles Lindbergh knew this: it was in pursuit of the $25,000 Orteig Prize that he made the first solo flight across the Atlantic. The creators of the Ansari X Prize, the $10 million award for the first nongovernmental manned space flight of a reusable craft, know it too. So do the folks at Google, whose $20 million Google Lunar X Prize will go to the first team that successfully lands and operates a rover on the moon.

Although "recognition awards" like the Nobel Prize honor work that's been done, "challenge awards" like the X Prizes (slogan: "Revolution Through Competition") spur the creation of what does not yet exist. A challenge award is more than just a goal statement with a grant of money. It is a grant of *permission:* to attack or reframe a problem any way possible. And it uses the evolutionary might of competition to allow great solutions to emerge bottom-up.

Challenge awards typically are tied to very specific technological goals—goals that are measurable and finite, even if audacious and far off. The specificity of the goal in the Ansari X Prize draws people to compete fiercely for it. But this can also be the challenge with challenge awards: by focusing so much on a discrete goal, such as manned space flight, they also narrow the field of rewarded endeavor and leave unacknowledged more pedestrian needs and deficits.

Consider, for comparison, a prize recently created by the Buckminster Fuller Institute with the charter "to support the development and implementation of a strategy that has significant potential to solve humanity's most pressing problems." Now, *that's* a challenge. The vision of the BFI prize is to beckon forth from any field, whether the arts or economics or basic science, what Fuller called a trimtab—"a catalyst inserted into a failing system at the right time and place that accelerates the transition to an equitable and sustainable future." Entrants have come up with ideas for carbon-neutral development of Appalachia, for education of the rural poor in India, for ways to make energy from dirt.

The BFI Challenge is much harder to categorize than the X Prize because its parameters are broad and the ideas it attracts may not be executable by a single party or team. This is precisely what is powerful about the challenge. It sparks new goals. What if there was a great prize for the first team to reduce violent gun deaths to zero in a given city? What if there was a prize for the development of a *social* technology—a ritual, a game, a curriculum—that would lead to a vast increase in the number of girls studying math or that would bring voter turnout to 100 percent? What if there was a prize for an online tool or a face-to-face experience that could generate lasting empathy for one's traditional enemies?

Inventing a good challenge—imagining it, naming it as such—is in many ways more important than inventing a good solution. Lincoln Center Institute has created an Imagination Award to honor schools that "incorporate imaginative thinking across the curriculum." There are criteria but no "perfect" answer or "typical" winner; just a rich array of possible ways to meet the challenge.

At the University of Southern California, a computer science graduate student named Christopher Leung, after working with a group of blind students, realized how poorly served such students were by the landscape of everyday technology. So he created a competition to catalyze new software programs that help the disabled expand their capabilities.

The competition, run now by a nonprofit called Project: Possibility, occurs during two intense days of code creation and attracts competing teams from around the country. The winning entrant in 2007 was a program that allows blind shoppers to aim a cell phone at supermarket shelves and hear a description of products and prices. Other entrants used software to allow paraplegics to move computer cursors with their thoughts. Project: Possibility aims next to create an open-source platform where people with disabilities can collaborate with software developers—to concoct not just new solutions but new challenges.

When we reward imagination in the setting of goals, great things—innovations—will likely emerge. But the true payoff is not the thing, however spectacular; it is the new ecosystem of possibility that makes such a thing even imaginable.

We need, then, to incentivize people to take the subpar social arrangements that we treat as givens here on Earth, and convert them into the stuff of big transformative goals. We need a contest not about how to achieve a stated goal but about how to state our goals more audaciously.

The X Prize, when you get down to it, is focused on the back end of the ICI Continuum: it's about the innovation. How about an X Prize for new X Prizes? An "X Prize Squared" would focus on the front end: it would cultivate the imagination. Try creating one yourself, for whatever ecosystem you want to transform. The great thing is, you don't need to be a rocket scientist to do it.

Break the Hand

Unschool yourself periodically

B y the time the 1980s arrived, Brice Marden was in need of something new. He had already achieved renown as one of the great Minimalist painters of the previous decade. With a precise blend of melted beeswax, paint, and turpentine, he created large monochrome panels that became his signature. Subtle, exacting, muted and granular, the panels defined him.

Until they didn't. Until, that is, he decided to stop making them and to stop painting altogether. Marden traveled around Thailand, India, and Sri Lanka, and when he returned, both to New York and to painting, his style had evolved dramatically. His work now bore the mark of Asia, in long looping expressive figures that resembled calligraphy and in crisscrossing patterns, of the sort he'd observed on seashells, that could be "read" in different directions.

Even more notably, Marden now painted and drew not with a brush or pen but with long, thin *sticks*. In his celebrated *Cold Mountain* series of paintings, etchings, and drawings, created in the late 1980s and inspired by Tang dynasty poems, Marden used those sticks to create scratchy, nearly random tangles of line, thought, and expression. He took twigs from his backyard or from his travels. He adjusted the length of the sticks to create different kinds of marks. The resulting works appear to be the products of another artist altogether.

Why? Why such a radical departure in style and method? Marden describes what he did as "breaking the hand." There is a literal sense in which using the stick, this new tool, required him to deprogram the muscle memory of wielding more traditional implements and to learn anew how to make an image with his hand. "By getting farther away, with a delicate instrument," he has observed, "in a way it becomes close: the slightest move is reflected."

But it's the figurative sense of "breaking the hand" that lingers. Marden came to see that the point of achieving mastery is not to stamp out repeat performances *ad infinitum* but rather to recycle the mastery and to express it in new ways. Starting over like this was not truly starting over: Marden's instincts, his skills, his years of abstracting his craft were all in him. "Everything that I ever put on the canvas is still there," he once said. "There's no way I could ever get rid of it."

A painter sees for a living. Experimenting with sticks, and applying all that accrued instinct and practice to a new genus of creation, was the way Brice Marden chose to refresh his sight. As remarkable and unique as his creations are, they remind us that we *all* see for a living—and that from time to time, we would all do well to break the hand.

Yes and . . .

Never say no to an idea

Three actors onstage, no script.

Player 1: It was awful, I tell you. There were birds everywhere!

Player 2: Yes—and I was wearing my brand-new bread suit. I couldn't even leave my front porch!

Player 3: And you think I'm henpecked.

Rule number one of improv: Always go to *Yes and*—no matter how weird or nonsensical or even prosaic the line you've just been handed. Never shut the flow with a *No* or even a *Yes, but.*

It's obvious why this rule makes the wheel of comedic improvisation go round and round. It should also be obvious why it's a good rule for life. For one thing, it requires that you actually listen closely to the people around you, instead of just waiting for them to finish so you can say your piece. Try it at the office, or at dinner. You'll notice less defensiveness, more surprise. For another thing, *Yes and* creates an environment where everyone in a group becomes invested in keeping a thing aloft—a shift in polarity from atomization to alignment.

But *Yes and* matters for our purposes because it activates the very forces that fuel the imagination. Imagination— the ability to conceive of what is not—is fundamentally about making associations and analogies between things that hadn't previously seemed connected. So a mind primed to make connections is a mind that literally can imagine more. Your synapses needn't fire as snappily as they do in great improv; what matters is whether, as a default, you are open to making one idea stitch to the last and to the next.

Yes and works also because idea generation is a classic instance of what scientists call network effects. The first few people to get a fax machine didn't derive much value from their investment until *many more* people got a fax machine: the network, not the individual machine, was the source of the value. In the generation of ideas, similarly, there are increasing returns to scale, and the denser the network the more exponentially rich the result. *Yes and* creates a denser network of ideas. It folds voices in. It allows the imagination—individual or collective—to take full advantage of diverse perspectives, to generate new blends, to make interesting use of blind spots or misunderstandings.

Yes and enables you also to stay focused on process rather than on end results. Viola Spolin, in her book *Improvisation for the Theater,* describes "the planned How" as taboo. For a good game of improvisation, she writes, Where and Who and What must be defined beforehand. "How the game can go can be known only when the players are out on the field," emphasizes Spolin. "Pre-planning how to do something throws the players into 'performance.'" And a focus on performance—on how you think others think you're doing—blocks the spontaneity and openness of true learning.

Mark Roth, the scientist who has discovered ways to suspend animation, says something similar. As he began to play with toxic gases in order to induce states of not-quite-deadness in mice and small mammals, he realized that in science there are always two distinct things to consider: a phenomenon that exists, like gravity; and how it works. "Most people in science," he notes, "work on the second." The how. Roth works on the phenomenon itself. He knows that his toxic cocktails can suspend animation. He doesn't know quite how. And he doesn't let that stop him from exploring, experimenting, and imagining ways to apply this learning in novel ways (say, with mammals like us).

Finally, *Yes and* teaches us something about how to fail well. Whether we're comedic actors or MacArthur geniuses or leaders of groups, don't we all need more practice at that? Yes—and that will be the next, and final, practice.

Fail Well

Treat failure like a skill

M any people run from failure. But what if we befriend it? What if, when failure arrives at our doorstep, we invite it in for a chat and get to know it? When we are toddlers, exploring the world around us, trying to see what works how and why, failure becomes our ally, our teacher. When we let failure guide us, we see a far wider field of possibility: now the realms where failure might lurk are not dangerous or unwelcoming; they are potentially useful.

Why do grown-ups so easily forget that?

Richard Lewis wonders. He sits every day with children and learns deeply from them as they make poems and paintings and wondrous myths about the unseen. Lewis is founder of The Touchstone Center for Children, an arts education organization he has run since 1969 in New

York City, and from where he sits, it is pretty clear what makes young humans allergic to imagination: school.

"In school," he says, "children begin to see that there are right and wrong answers and that rewards come with the right answers. This produces the sense that the real achievement of mind is being right." Lewis is not some utopian who rails against any distinction between the correct and the incorrect. "But you've got to discern," he insists, "between those parts where correct answers matter, like spelling and math, and all those other parts where it does *not*."

When we are children, our learning is not linear or category-minded or geared to success. It just *is*. As we fiddle with magnets or listen to the night or trudge across snow, we see, we wonder, we try—we try a different way. But eventually we get contaminated with this notion of "for every question, a right answer." And from there we become fearful of error—of failure. We want to align the core of our identity to a true north of correctness.
So we strive mightily every minute to stave off wrongness. We marshal the full might of our self-justification machinery to lay errors and failures at the feet of others: *Mistakes Were Made,* as the title of Carol Tavris and Elliot Aronson's book puts it (subtitle: *But Not by* Me).

as possible to the realm of "right" answers. Most of life is judgment calls, not binary choices. Failure, properly consumed, fortifies judgment.

Adults, especially parents, understand that it is part of our responsibility to point out to children their bad habits. Imagine if all children had the vocabulary to point out our bad habits to us. But wait a minute—they do. They may not use spoken words. They use a kind of sign language. Each motion offers a lesson in failing well: *Here Dad, look—this is how to persist at figuring something out.* Or: *Here's how it looks when you try something without assuming you'll stink at it.* A child's gestures and postures add up to a tale told in symbols, inviting us to fill the gaps on our own. Just as in sign language. Or poetry.

One day, in a classroom in East Harlem, Richard Lewis asked a group of seven- and eight-year-olds, "Do you think there is a bird who could make the rain fall, or who could bring up the sun in the sky?" They talked about what that bird would be, would look like, would do, and he asked them to draw it. Then he asked the children to describe their visions. This is what Joel, one of those children, said:

> *My bird comes out at night on a full moon. He flies through the sky. At night you can never see him. He is in you. His name is imagination. He lives in a*

place called heart brain body. It is in everyone. Some
adults think it is childish but it will never leave you
even if you hide it.

The truly unconscionable failure is to cage that bird.
Everything else is possible.

part Three

The Purposes

Conclusion

You'll remember that in the introduction to this field manual, we laid out a framework to explain why we say "imagination first."

The ICI Continuum, as we call it—in which imagination begets creativity, and creativity begets innovation—is more than a piece of shorthand. It is a point of view about what matters most. It is an argument about how any effective approach to change, improvement, reform, or reinvention—of *anything*—must begin with a full development of the habits of imagination. There is no innovation when the imagination is starved. Period.

If we are out of shape physically, we can't expect to become fit in a sudden burst. We may wish otherwise, and we may succumb to pills or procedures or pitches that promise immediate results. And every time, we learn the hard way. It takes regimen, repetition, nutrition, discipline. It takes time. It takes practice.

In this conclusion, we want to review what we mean by practice. We'll look at some of the themes that have arisen throughout our twenty-eight-and-a-half practices. We'll consider the conundrum of how to "routinize" imagination, especially in larger-scale groups and organizations. And we'll end with a reflection on the *purposes* to which we put our unleashed imagination.

How to *What If*

The art of *What if* is just that: an art. It does not reside in a self-contained set of mathematical axioms. There are no Newtonian principles waiting to be codified. There is only this: raw human experience, as filtered through the imperfect and bias-ridden screens of our ability to perceive; a sense of grammar, as patterns emerge; and practice, as we commit to it.

You run a business and you are losing customers and market share to your largest competitor. You learn that a third firm wants to enter the market via a merger with either your company or the competitor. Merging could mean shedding jobs; not merging could mean bankruptcy. Is there another way?

You have slipped into a vicious circle of mistrust with your teenage son. He has decided that everything you have to say is a form of judgment, and has stopped telling you anything of substance about his life. This makes you only more inclined to ask questions that sound to him like judgment. Is there another way?

You've been asked by your fellow citizens to lead the creation of a renewal plan for the city's downtown. You collect great new ideas. But when it's time for concrete changes, there are fiefs to defend, interests to balance, taxes to raise. You find yourself now the steward of a plan for timid, incremental change—and yet you are attacked as if you were proposing revolution. Is there another way?

Earlier in this book, we shared Lincoln Center Institute's Capacities for Imaginative Learning. We believe they capture the essence of the art of *What if*. The Capacities are used across the school curriculum, but were designed originally for use with works of art. That's still how they can be used—particularly if you notice everything around you as you would a work of art. Including *you*: your dilemmas, your choices, your search for a better way. Your community of practice, your tribe of fellow travelers. It's worth revisiting those capacities now:

- Noticing deeply

- Embodying

- Questioning

- Identifying patterns

- Making connections

- Exhibiting empathy

- Creating meaning

- Taking action

- Reflecting and assessing

Applying these Capacities to something from your life experience—or from a group's shared experience—is a great way to warm up the imagination. The "object of study" can be anything—a challenge or conflict or opportunity, drawn from a hard conversation with a family member, say; or a new initiative you're trying to get launched at work; or your involvement in a group that needs to recruit new members. Resist the impulse to "solve" anything. Just treat that object of study like an object of study—a case, a specimen, a still life. What do you notice? How does it feel? What questions arise, and what patterns emerge?

Having warmed up this way, return to the practices of this book and start using them. The cross-connections will become clear. What is Cloud Appreciation but noticing deeply, questioning, and identifying patterns? What is Playing Telephone but making connections, creating meaning, and taking action? What is Swapping

Bodies but exhibiting empathy, reflecting, and assessing? What is Breaking the Hand but embodying an experience through sense and emotion? Think of each practice as a form of exercise, which is to say, repeated combinations and extrapolations of the moves you did in warm-ups.

The key to making the practices meaningful is, quite simply, *practice*. Let's say one of our practices speaks powerfully to you. Say you try it. Say it helps you get past an emotional block or a negative narrative or a situation of stuckness. Your imagination expands. You will be thrilled. You will want to think you're done. You will be wrong. Sooner or later, you will need to practice some more.

Practice, in every sense of the word, is not about reaching "doneness"; it's about staying loose and doing it again. The analogy to exercise is total: if you regularly swim or run or do meditative breathing, there is no moment when you "finish" getting fit and no longer need effort to sustain it. Nor is there any way to elevate your abilities without continuous practice. The good news, then, is that imagination is a muscle: it can be toned and strengthened. The bad news is that imagination is a muscle: neglecting it leads to atrophy and enervation.

So what's the best way to ensure imaginative fitness? Well, think about the best way to stay committed to *any* workout regimen. You do it with others.

The Networked Imagination

We did not write this book in order to help individual readers in isolation. Even though all the practices can be used in very personal ways, this is not meant to be a self-help book. It is meant to be a *"selves*-help" book. We believe it's in the *collective* arena that imagination can do the most—for good *or* for ill.

Let's return to an example we mentioned in the introduction, the report of the 9/11 Commission. In the Commission's view, one of the great failures of the intelligence agencies before 9/11 was a failure to *institutionalize* imagination. Scenarios in which aircraft were hijacked for use as weapons against the United States had been developed here and there across the government's security agencies. But never were the scattered scenarios connected into an actionable pattern. Bureaucrats trudged along, blinders on. As historian Gordon Prange said of comparable failures pre-Pearl Harbor, "In the face of a clear warning, alert measures bowed to routine."

And so in its report the 9/11 Commission called urgently for "routinizing, even bureaucratizing, the exercise of imagination." That may sound like an oxymoron, if we take "routine" to mean mindless reflex. But if we take "routine" instead to mean mindful practice, it is decidedly not an oxymoron. In fact, thinking about the Commission's suggestions is a pretty good way to illuminate the most common blind spots of imagination, on both an individual and institutional scale.

Our human habits of self-delusion are legion. What we think we see seems pretty clear, until we realize that what we think is what we see. We tend to interpret new information in ways that bend toward our preconceptions and confirm them. We believe that *we* see things "as they really are" but that everyone else's vision is clouded. We resolve cognitive dissonance in the most self-justifying manner available. Then we develop a tunnel vision that impedes our ability to empathize and switch shoes with someone. Especially an enemy.

Each of these tendencies shapes how we move in the world as individuals. But their power is magnified *exponentially* when we move in the world *as groups.* That's why cultivating imagination in an organization or community is not a simple matter of multiplying personal practice by a thousand or by a million. Scale distorts. It requires different mindsets and metaphors altogether. Imagination is not a mass-produced commodity. It is a natural resource that waters every environment we move in. The larger and more complex the environment, the greater the effort required to harness that resource for all.

In 2000, Procter & Gamble took the radical step of opening its vast trove of patents, making them available to anyone for a licensing fee, and then told its executives to start generating at least half their new product ideas from beyond the walls of P&G. As a result, its leaders have had to learn that success within the company depends on fostering success outside the company. The Marine Corps' training doctrine, sharpened by two wars, trains unit leaders at the lowest level to think, to improvise, to imagine new solutions without waiting for HQ to give direction in combat. As their doctrinal manuals on warfighting intone, "Marine Corps maneuver warfare philosophy is based on a decentralized command environment that requires decisive squad leaders."

Both P&G and the Marine Corps have, in effect, created open-source operating systems. So has the Exploratorium, the pioneering and frenetically interactive science museum inSan Francisco. Created in 1969, the Exploratorium still embodies the bottom-up, countercultural spirit of its founders. If you have an idea for a new exhibit, and take the time to make a little model of the exhibit, you can come and pitch the concept to a staff team at the museum that includes scientists, artists, and machinists. It doesn't matter if you're the janitor at the Exploratorium, the executive director, or even a first-time visitor. If the team likes the concept, they'll build a prototype right away. Then they'll put it on the floor for the public to try out. The staff will observe people playing with the prototype. They'll take notes and make adjustments, refine the directions or the flow of the experience. If the public responds well, the exhibit is a keeper. Just like that.

To routinize imagination in an open-source environment is not to issue top-down commands ("Be more imaginative!") or to dictate outcomes. It is to set high-level challenges and then allow evolution to yield the hardiest possibilities and solutions. It is to create an ecosystem where good ideas can emerge from anywhere. Most of all, it is to ensure that throughout the ecosystem even the smallest units of operation have a shared idea of what the goal is and what constitutes good practice.

Think, if you will, in terms of epidemics. What are the initial environmental conditions that enable a virus to live and spread? How do institutions act to make people more or less susceptible to the virus? When the virus first spreads, what are we taught to do to contain it? How are we told this?

Now, imagine that the virus is imagination. Instead of trying to contain the virus, imagine what you'd do to accelerate its spread. How would you nurture its earliest forms? What would you do to lower the community's resistance to it? How would you help the virus adapt to anti-imagination treatments and to grow even fiercer?

The goal for any healthy organization is to create epidemics of imagination.

Trust is vital. Indeed, trust is the *only* way that imagination can ever become routine in an organization. Which is why *every* practice we've suggested in this field manual is designed to foster trust. Trust in every direction—peer to peer, leader to follower, after failure, after success—enables groups to become self-aware without self-consciousness, to identify blind spots without defensiveness, to correct and adapt without direction.

Trust also enables a group to take advantage of the increasingly networked nature of the world. The Internet is a network. Your memory is a network. To a generation growing up on Facebook, *I* is a network and so is *we*. Link by link, the idea of the network now dominates the popular imagination. Which is helpful, because imagination itself is but a network: a generative web of association, memory, and meme. And like any robust network, imagination *scales sideways* without control rather than hierarchically with.

For Good

There is, alas, a dark side to all this. Few contemporary organizations, for instance, have been more effective at scaling imagination sideways than al Qaeda. They made a

In our desperate ego-coddling efforts to fend off failure and inch toward power, we do two costly things: First, we hug the status quo tight, because that is the rational way to avoid the cognitive dissonance of being possibly wrong or a fool or a failure. Second, we forget what children know intuitively, which is that there's a useful way to fail and a wasteful way. The *wasteful* way to fail is to deny it or hide it. This is what the theater director Bartlett Sher calls "aggressive stupidity"—a firing offense in his companies, but par for the course in many others. The *useful* way is to treat failing like a learnable skill—something that, with effort and reflection, we can get better at until one day we can reach the point of mastery. *If at first you don't fail, try, try again.*

How do we become masters at failing? For one thing, practice. Whether in Olympic swimming or Army field exercises, corporate crisis management or piano lessons, good practice is not mere repetition; it is paying attention. It is releasing the ego's hold on the situation long enough to let our mistakes guide us. It is creating a safe environment where others can learn the same way. We get better at failure by not punishing it when it's useful. And what makes it more likely to be useful is wielding Lewis's rule of discernment like a fine-edged knife against the clay of experience, surrendering as little hardy meme that can survive in many environments. They invented a networked operating system that can operate in almost any milieu and that inspires the creation of locally relevant applications.

Indeed, there is a dark side to every single practice we have detailed in these pages. Narratives can be reshaped to hold peoples captive. Counterfactuals can be used to stir prejudice. The hoarding of bits can be used to fashion vast conspiracy theories. Quests can be created to feed our basest desires.

Imagination is like fire. No—strike that. Imagination *is* fire. By reading this field manual, you've perhaps figured out a few ways to make sparks and fan flames. Now comes the question: To what ends shall you use that fire?

Rosamund Zander is a psychotherapist and co-author of *The Art of Possibility*, a celebrated and influential book about the practice of imagination. Zander forms what she calls "accomplishment groups"—circles of people who meet regularly over the course of a year, each of them committing to pursue and achieve a deep, imaginative goal. The goal can be professional or personal, public or private. Whatever the goal may be, implicit in the endeavor—and reinforced by the norms of the group—is the expectation that the project be *good*.

Having such an expectation is like having a giant magnet that pulls together the stray filaments of chance and circumstance. Consider the chef Jerilyn Brusseau. Jerilyn's brother Daniel was a helicopter pilot in the Vietnam War. He was killed by the enemy in Quang Tri Province. That is why Jerilyn founded an organization called PeaceTrees Vietnam, which decommissions land mines and unexploded ordnance in Quang Tri Province, and plants trees in their place.

"That is why" may sound not quite right to you. It seems oversimplified. But it captures exactly the essence of what happened: tragedy struck. Brusseau imagined a way to transform it into something constructive. Something constructive happened. It was her imagination that gave the unfolding of these events the force of direct causation. And it was the fact that her imagination was oriented to *positive* purpose that gave this chain of events a beneficial result.

Every one of us every day faces situations, whether tragic or joyous or trivial, that activate the imagination. In choosing *how* we want to activate it, we either add to or subtract from the sum total of good in the world. Do we deploy our imagination for the accumulation of power? The avoidance of pain? The eliding of responsibility? The reinforcement of pathology? The erosion of morals?

The world we inhabit is, in Oliver Wendell Holmes's phrase, "the witness and external deposit" of our interior imaginative life. It is nothing more. The categories and distinctions we use to demarcate possible and impossible, worthy or unworthy, are but mental traditions, made by man and endowed by time with mystical significance. People like us created those categories. People like us can uncreate them. We can convert land mines into trees.

Will we always accomplish what we imagine? Of course not. But we will certainly never accomplish what we refuse to imagine.

Read the headlines today. Now read them again, as if they were from last year. You realize in that moment of detachment that there was nothing foreordained about these particular headlines. Why did it have to be that violence broke out again in the Middle East? Why did it have to be that so many children around the globe succumbed to easily preventable diseases? Why did it have to be that our political leaders spent so much time raising money for campaigns?

In that moment of detachment it becomes evident that "because it's always been that way" is the answer that comes from too much knowledge, from path dependence and path acceptance. If we want to contemplate—let alone generate—a vastly different set of headlines, we have to rekindle a youthful naivete, a willful bewilderment about all the insanity and inadequacy that we come to tolerate, and a child's habit of letting thought experiments run and run.

"You cannot depend on your eyes," said Mark Twain, "when your imagination is out of focus." In these pages we've offered some new ways to see seeing. Now it's up to you to find some new ways to do doing.

To change the world at any scale—even a scale of one—demands a lot. It demands the determination to see a vision through to execution. It demands deep applied understanding of how to move ideas and people across networks and systems. It demands mass and might and relentless effort.

But before any of this, changing yourself and the world demands a purpose-fed, positively charged, playful imagination.

It demands imagination first.

For Further
Exploration

Here is a selection of the many works and sources that have inspired us, shaped our thinking, and sparked our imagination. Please check our Web site, imaginationfirst.com, for updated lists and references!

Books

Ackerman, Diane. *Deep Play*. New York: Vintage, 1999.

Anderson, Benedict. *Imagined Communities*. New York: Verso, 1983.

Arnheim, Rudolph. *Visual Thinking*. Berkeley: University of California Press, 1969.

Barry, Lynda. *What It Is*. Montreal: Drawn & Quarterly, 2008.

Berns, Gregory. *Iconoclast: A Neuroscientist Reveals How to Think Differently.* Boston: Harvard Business School Press, 2008.

Beveridge, W. I. B. *The Art of Scientific Investigation.* New York: Norton, 1957.

Blumenthal, Eileen, Julie Taymor, and Antonio Monda. *Julie Taymor: Playing with Fire.* New York: Abrams, 1999.

Brosterman, Norman. *Inventing Kindergarten.* New York: Abrams, 1997.

Brown, John Seely, and Paul Duguid. *The Social Life of Information.* Boston: Harvard Business School Press, 2000.

Campbell, Joseph. *The Hero with a Thousand Faces.* Princeton: Princeton University Press, 1949.

Chodorow, Joan, ed. *Jung on Active Imagination.* Princeton: Princeton University Press, 1997.

Cialdini, Robert. *Influence.* Boston: Scott, Foresman, 1988.

Coles, Robert. *The Call of Stories: Teaching and the Moral Imagination.* Boston: Houghton Mifflin, 1989.

Csikszentmihalyi, Mihaly. *Flow: The Psychology of Optimal Experience.* New York: Harper & Row, 1990.

Dewey, John. *Experience and Education.* New York: Touchstone, 1938.

Dweck, Carol S. *Mindset: The New Psychology of Success.* New York: Random House, 2006.

Eberle, Bob. *Scamper: Creative Games and Activities for Imagination Development.* Waco, TX: Prufrock Press, 1996.

Egan, Kieran. *An Imaginative Approach to Teaching.* San Francisco: Jossey-Bass, 2005.

Eisner, Elliot W. *The Educational Imagination: On the Design and Evaluation of School Programs.* New York: Macmillan, 1994.

Finke, Ronald. *Creative Imagery: Discoveries and Inventions in Visualization.* Hillsdale, NJ: Erlbaum, 1990.

Fisher, Roger, and William Ury. *Getting to Yes: Negotiating Agreement Without Giving In.* New York: Penguin, 1981.

Frye, Northrop. *The Educated Imagination.* Bloomington: Indiana University Press, 1964.

Gallwey, Timothy. *The Inner Game of Tennis.* New York: Random House, 1974.

Gardner, Howard. *Frames of Mind: The Theory of Multiple Intelligences.* New York: Perseus Books, 1983.

Gentner, Dedre, Keith J. Holyoak, and Boicho N. Kokinov, eds. *The Analogical Mind: Perspectives from Cognitive Science.* Cambridge, MA: MIT Press, 2001.

Gilbert, Daniel. *Stumbling on Happiness*. New York: Knopf, 2006.

Gladwell, Malcolm. *Outliers: The Story of Success*. New York: Little, Brown, 2009.

Gopnik, Alison. *The Philosophical Baby*. New York: Farrar, Straus & Giroux, 2009.

Gopnik, Alison, and Andrew N. Meltzoff. *Words, Thoughts, and Theories*. Cambridge, MA: MIT Press, 1997.

Greene, Maxine. *Releasing the Imagination*. San Francisco: Jossey-Bass, 1995.

Greene, Maxine. *Variations on a Blue Guitar*. New York: Teachers College Press, 2001.

Harris, Paul L. *The Work of the Imagination*. Malden, MA: Blackwell, 2000.

Hofstadter, Douglas. *I Am a Strange Loop*. New York: Basic Books, 2007.

Hyde, Lewis. *The Gift: Creativity and the Artist in the Modern World*. New York: Vintage, 1979.

Imagineers, The. *The Imagineering Way: Ideas to Ignite Your Creativity*. New York: Disney Editions, 2003.

Kao, John. *Innovation Nation: How America Is Losing Its Innovation Edge, Why It Matters, and What We Can Do to Get It Back*. New York: Free Press, 2007.

Kuhn, Thomas. *The Structure of Scientific Revolutions.* Chicago: University of Chicago Press, 1962.

Lakoff, George, and Mark Johnson. *Metaphors We Live By.* Chicago: University of Chicago Press, 1980.

Lehrer, Jonah. *Proust Was a Neuroscientist.* New York: Mariner Books, 2007.

Lewis, Richard. *Living by Wonder: The Imaginative Life of Childhood.* New York: Touchstone Center Publications, 1998.

Lienhard, John H. *How Invention Begins: Echoes of Old Voices in the Rise of New Machines.* New York: Oxford University Press, 2006.

MacKenzie, Gordon. *Orbiting the Giant Hairball.* New York: Viking, 1996.

Martin, Steve. *Born Standing Up.* New York: Scribner, 2007.

Moss, Robert. *The Three "Only" Things: Tapping the Power of Dreams, Coincidence, and Imagination.* Novato, CA: New World Library, 2007.

National Commission on Terrorist Attacks upon the United States. *The 9/11 Commission Report.* New York: Norton, 2004.

Nelms, Henning. *Magic and Showmanship.* Mineola, NY: Dover, 1969.

Osborn, Alex. *Applied Imagination.* New York: Scribner, 1953.

Palmer, Parker. *The Courage to Teach*. San Francisco: Jossey-Bass, 1998.

Papert, Seymour. *Mindstorms: Children, Computers, and Powerful Ideas*. New York: Perseus, 1993.

Pink, Daniel. *A Whole New Mind*. New York: Riverhead, 2005.

Pinker, Steven. *How the Mind Works*. New York: Norton, 1997.

Ramachandran, V. S. *A Brief Tour of Human Consciousness*. New York: Pi Press, 2004.

Robinson, Ken. *Out of Our Minds: Learning to Be Creative*. West Sussex, UK: Capstone, 2000.

Ryle, Gilbert. *Concept of Mind*. New York: Hutchinson's University Library, 1949.

Salen, Katie, and Eric Zimmerman. *Rules of Play: Game Design Fundamentals*. Cambridge: MIT Press, 2004.

Sartre, Jean-Paul. *The Psychology of Imagination*. Secaucus, NJ: Citadel, 1948.

Sawyer, Keith. *Group Genius: The Creative Power of Collaboration*. New York: Basic Books, 2007.

Schön, Donald. *The Reflective Practitioner: How Professionals Think in Action*. New York: Basic Books, 1983.

Spolin, Viola. *Improvisation for the Theater*. Evanston, IL: Northwestern University Press, 1963.

Sternberg, Robert J., ed. *Handbook of Creativity*. New York: Cambridge University Press, 1999.

Taleb, Nassim Nicholas. *The Black Swan*. New York: Random House, 2007.

Tavris, Carol, and Elliot Aronson. *Mistakes Were Made (But Not by Me)*. New York: Harcourt, 2007.

Tharp, Twyla. *The Creative Habit: Learn It and Use It for Life*. New York: Simon & Schuster, 2003.

Tufte, Edward. *Visual Explanations*. Cheshire, CT: Graphics Press, 1997.

U.S. Army-Marine Corps Counterinsurgency Field Manual. Chicago: University of Chicago Press, 2007.

Warnock, Mary. *Imagination*. Berkeley: University of California Press, 1976.

Watts, Alan. *Still the Mind: An Introduction to Meditation*. Novato, CA: New World Library, 2000.

Woolf, Virginia. *A Room of One's Own*. New York: Harvest Books, 2005.

Yamashita, Keith, and Sandra Spataro. *Unstuck*. New York: Portfolio, 2004.

Yergin, Daniel, and Thane Gustafson. *Russia 2010 and What It Means for the World*. New York: Random House, 1993.

Zander, Rosamund Stone, and Benjamin Zander. *The Art of Possibility*. New York: Penguin, 2002.

Articles

Amabile, Teresa. "How to Kill Creativity." *Harvard Business Review*, September-October 1998, 77–87.

Amabile, Teresa, and Mukti Khaire. "Creativity and the Role of the Leader." *Harvard Business Review*, October 2008, 100.

Anderson, P. W. "More Is Different." *Science*, August 4, 1972, 393.

Carey, Benedict. "Anticipating the Future to 'See' the Present." *New York Times*, June 10, 2008, D5.

Carey, Benedict. "Standing in Someone Else's Shoes." *New York Times*, December 2, 2008, D5.

Churchill, Winston S. "If Lee Had Not Won the Battle of Gettysburg." *Scribner's Magazine*, December 1930. Reprinted in *Collected Essays, IV*, 7–84.

Clendaniel, Morgan. "Fall Down Go Boom." *Good*, September-October 2008, 84.

Flanigan, James. "Creating Software That Opens Worlds to the Disabled." *New York Times*, December 18, 2008, B7.

Goetz, Thomas. "Mind the Gaps." *Wired*, October 2007, 31.

Greene, Maxine. "Art and Imagination: Reclaiming the Sense of Possibility." *Phi Delta Kappan*, January 1, 1995.

Holmes, Oliver Wendell Jr. "The Path of the Law." *10 Harvard Law Review 457*, 1897.

Holzer, Madeleine Fuchs. Capacities for Imaginative Learning, in *Aesthetic Education, Inquiry, and the Imagination. "Teaching and Learning at Lincoln Center Institute."* Lincoln Center Institute, 2005.

Lehrer, Jonah. "A New State of Mind." *Seed*, July-August 2008, 65.

Ouellette, Jeannine. "The Death and Life of the American Imagination." *The Rake*, November 2007.

"Scientific American Reports: Special Edition on Perception," *Scientific American*, July 15, 2008.

Shaw, Jonathan. "The Physics of the Familiar." *Harvard Magazine*, March-April 2008, 45.

Sternberg, Robert. "Creativity Is a Habit." *Education Week*, February 22, 2006, 47–64.

Stickgold, Robert, and Jeffrey M. Ellenbogen. "Quiet! Sleeping Brain at Work." *Scientific American Mind*, August-September 2008, 23.

Other Individuals and Organizations Referenced in the Book

Paula Boggs, musician and lawyer: www.myspace.com/paulaboggs

Zach Brock, violinist: www.zachbrock.com

Jerilyn Brusseau, PeaceTrees Vietnam: www.peacetreesvietnam.org

John Seely Brown, author: www.johnseelybrown.com

Geoffrey Canada, Harlem Children's Zone: www.hcz.org

Cloud Appreciation Society: www.cloudappreciationsociety.org

Bonnie Dunbar, The Museum of Flight: www.museumofflight.org

Carol Dweck, Stanford University: www-psych.stanford.edu/~dweck/

14/48 Theater Festival: www.1448fest.com

Nick Fortugno, Rebel Monkey: www.rebelmonkey.com

Buckminster Fuller Institute: www.bfi.org

Alison Gopnik, University of California, Berkeley: www.alisongopnik.com

David Gonzalez, storyteller: www.davidgonzalez.com

Maxine Greene, Lincoln Center Institute: www.
lcinstitute.org

Harvard Negotiation Project: www.pon.harvard.edu/
research/projects/hnp.php3

Eric Haseltine, Haseltine Partners: www.leighbureau.
com/speaker.asp?id=431

David Herskovits, Target Margin Theater: www.
targetmargin.org

Hollyhock Retreat Centre: www.hollyhock.ca

Chris Jordan, photographer: www.chrisjordan.com

Luke Keller, Ithaca College: http://faculty.ithaca.edu/
lkeller/

Richard Lewis, Touchstone Center for Children:
www.touchstonecenter.net

Tod Machover, MIT Media Lab: www.media.mit.edu/
people/bio_tod.html

Brice Marden, painter: www.diaart.org/exhibs/marden/
coldmountain/

David McConville, Elumenati: www.elumenati.com

MIT Media Lab: www.media.mit.edu

Oblique Strategies: www.rtqe.net/ObliqueStrategies/

Andrea Peterson, teacher: www.ccsso.org/projects/
national_teacher_of_the_year/national_teachers/
9842.cfm

V. S. Ramachandran, University of California, San Diego:
http://cbc.ucsd.edu/ramabio.html

David Rockwell, Rockwell Group: www.rockwellgroup.
com

Mark Roth, Fred Hutchinson Cancer Research Center:
http://labs.fhcrc.org/roth/

Katie Salen, Parsons The New School for Design:
www.gamersmob.com/

Bartlett Sher, Intiman Theater: www.intiman.org/About/
bsher.html

Julie Taymor, director: www.imdb.com/name/
nm0853380/

Twyla Tharp, choreographer: www.twylatharp.org

United States Marine Corps Officer Candidates School:
www.ocs.usmc.mil

Walt Disney Imagineering: http://corporate.
disney.go.com/careers/who_imagineering.html

Eric Walton, magician: www.ericwalton.com

X PRIZE Foundation:
http://space.xprize.org/ansari-x-prize

Benjamin Zander, conductor and teacher:
www.benjaminzander.com

Rosamund Zander, therapist and coach:
www.rosamundzander.com

Index

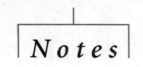

Notes

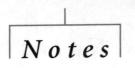

Notes

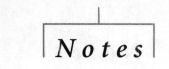

Notes

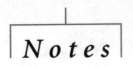

Notes

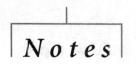

Notes

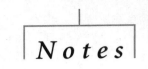

Notes